Anyone Can Evangelize

7 Decisions You Can Make to Kickstart a Habit of Sharing Jesus Daily

JESSE STIRNEMANN

Copyright © 2025 Jesse Stirnemann

All rights reserved. No part of this publication may be reproduced, distributed, or transmitted in any form or by any means, including photocopying, recording, or other electronic or mechanical methods, without the prior written permission of the publisher, except in the case of brief quotations embodied in critical reviews and certain other noncommercial uses permitted by copyright law. For permission requests, write to the publisher, addressed "Attention: Permissions Coordinator," to info@arrowpresspublishing.com

Paperback: 978-1-951475-41-3
Ebook: 978-1-951475-42-0

Library of Congress Control Number: 2024926185

First paperback edition: February 2025

Accounts in this book are written to the truest recollection of the author's memory. Some names, places, and identifying details have been changed to protect privacy.

All Scripture quotations, unless otherwise indicated, are taken from the Holy Bible, New International Version®, NIV®. Copyright ©1973, 1978, 1984, 2011 by Biblica, Inc.™ Used by permission of Zondervan. All rights reserved worldwide. www.zondervan.com. The "NIV" and "New InternationalVersion" are trademarks registered in the United States Patent and Trademark Office by Biblica, Inc.™

Scripture quotations marked NLT are taken from the Holy Bible, New Living Translation, copyright
©1996, 2004, 2015 by Tyndale House Foundation. Used by permission of Tyndale House Publishers,
a Division of Tyndale House Ministries, Carol Stream, Illinois 60188. All rights reserved.

Scripture quotations marked NKJV are taken from the New King James Version®. Copyright © 1982
by Thomas Nelson. Used by permission. All rights reserved.

Arrow Press Publishing
Summerville, SC 29486

www.arrowpresspublishing.com

"In his book, *Anyone Can Evangelize,* Jesse Stirnemann lays out a simple step-by-step process that makes fulfilling the Great Commission much easier to grasp. I highly recommend you grab a copy of this book, read through it, apply it, and watch God use your life as a tool to advance his kingdom."

– Chris Sonksen, Pastor/Speaker/Author/Coach

"Believers are called to share the good news of the gospel. *Anyone Can Evangelize* provides encouragement and instruction in sharing Christ with anyone. It's just what we need to help anyone share the gospel with confidence."

– Robert Brooks, Athletes in Action Pro Ministry Senior Staff

"This book is fresh, relevant, timely, full of personal encounters, and tons of scripture. You will discover how evangelism can be easier than you always feared if you simply start small. Start by reading this incredible book, a practical guide to everyday evangelism."

– Rev. Dr. George A. Johnson, Senior Pastor at Hope Community Baptist Church, Adjunct Professor at Detroit Bible Institute, Vice Moderator of the North American Baptist Conference

"This book imparts training that will help any believer to overcome roadblocks to evangelism as well as tools that can make Gospel conversations happen more naturally. We need more books like this in the Body of Christ!"

– Dustin Renz, President of Make Way Ministries

"Jesse speaks from personal experience, one with a deep concern for a fallen world and a tremendous desire to lead others to Jesus. This book is a needed practical resource for the church."

– Dr. David Blanchard, Author of *Let's Talk: Eleven Conversations for People Who Take Life, Faith, and the Church Seriously*

"If you have ignored or been too timid to share Jesus consistently, this thoughtful and insightful book is for you! In it, Pastor Jesse lays out a simple, seven-step approach to evangelism that any Christian can follow."

– Dr. Michael Davis, PhD in History from the University of Maryland, Retired with 35 Years of U.S. Active Military Service

Contents

Foreword by Kevin L. Crow	7
Spiritual Preparation	11
Introduction: Start Small	17
Decision #1: Believe	23
Decision #2: Pray	49
Decision #3: Love	71
Decision #4: Obey	87
Decision #5: Prepare	111
Decision #6: Relate	135
Decision #7: Speak - Part 1	149
Decision #7: Speak - Part 2	165
Conclusion: Do Not Give Up	193

Going Further

#1: Small Group Questions	203
#2: 7 Decisions to Lead Your Kids to Christ	205
#3: 7 Decisions to Create an Outreach Culture at your Church	211
Acknowledgements	217
Notes	221
Meet Jesse Stirnemann	227

Foreword

How do you know the character of a person? You watch what they do when no one is looking. What do they do when they don't get noticed, praised, or credit?

We were looking to hire a staff pastor for our church and I received one resume three times. Every time, after reading it, it hit the trash can. It just wasn't a good resume.

Then, one Sunday, a regular attender at our church approached me and said that there was this guy who witnessed to him one day at the beach. The approach that he described sounds like the same approach used in at least half a dozen stories in this book.

Anyone Can Evangelize

You might have guessed it. The person who had witnessed to the man from our church was Jesse Stirnemann. He was at the beach with his family and took time to try and make friends with a man so he could share Jesus with him.

There was no reason for Jesse to share Jesus with the man, other than the fact that he cared about his soul. I can work with that kind of character, so we wound up hiring Jesse as a staff pastor at our church.

I have come to realize that evangelism isn't just something Jesse believes we should do, it is a way of life for him. He is good at sharing Jesus with people.

If my car is broken, I don't take it to a mechanic whose car won't run. And, I don't ask an electrician to fix my wiring if the light switches in his house don't work. Similarly, I don't want marriage advice from someone getting divorced for the 5th time.

When it comes to instruction about how to share Jesus with the unsaved, it is wise to learn from someone who is successful at leading people to Christ.

As I read this book, I realized that I was reading a beginner's guide on how to lead people to Jesus. The content is applicable, and the stories are inspiring. As I like to say, Jesse puts the cookies on the bottom shelf so we all can get one.

Don't just read this book, apply it. And may God help you learn how to share your faith, because "Anyone can Evangelize."

Kevin L. Crow

Senior Pastor at Harvest Ridge Church

Spiritual Preparation

FOR *ANYONE CAN EVANGELIZE*

I am so glad you have decided to read a book all about how to share the Good News of Jesus Christ more effectively. I am excited for you to learn why it is true that anyone (including you) can *evangelize*!

However, I need to give you a *warning*.

You should expect opposition reading a book like this one. Three specific places will be sources of push back.

1. Yourself- You are facing off with some big fears. Evangelism takes a lot of self-denial. So do not be surprised when your flesh shakes its head at some of the points and pages.

2. People- Of course, you know that non-Christians can jeer or ignore the outreaching Christian. However, you may be surprised that even a believer will throw out a joke that you are being a "Jesus Freak" for reading a book on evangelism. Lukewarm Christians don't like when one catches fire.

3. Satan- He does not like Jesus, and He does not like when Christians start trying to rescue people from darkness. He will leave you alone until you start fighting against his kingdom. Do not be surprised if the evil one draws up a scheme against your effort to read *Anyone Can Evangelize*.

Earlier this year, I had an experience that cemented my desire to write this short preparatory section of this book. The week that I sat down to read a book on spiritual authority, I came under one of the most acute and annoying spiritual attacks of my life.

I felt as though I was underwater—physically ill and weighed down. Even my children were out of sorts by the end of the week.

Thankfully, I was able to recognize what was going on and take the necessary steps to *counteract* the attack.

1: Recognize it.
2: Take authority in Christ's name.
3: Ask for prayer from my church family.
4: Stand firm until it passed.

Do not be afraid. Walk in God's power and love on this learning journey. Enjoy the process and stick with it even when it's tough. God is with you every step of the way.

Let's say a prayer together as we begin:

Father,

Thank you for the opportunity to learn how to share Your story. Your Gospel has changed me, and I want to be used by You to impact others. If any attack or opposition comes as I set my mind to read this book, I ask, Jesus, that You would help me to identify and overcome it by the power of Your blood. Forgive my shortcomings in my personal witness and make me brave through the power of Your Spirit. Thank you for opening doors to use what I am learning, and thank you for this day and this moment with You.

In Jesus' Name,

Amen

Jesus Feeds the Five Thousand

Some time after this, Jesus crossed to the far shore of the Sea of Galilee (that is, the Sea of Tiberias), [2] and a great crowd of people followed him because they saw the signs he had performed by healing the sick. [3] Then Jesus went up on a mountainside and sat down with his disciples. [4] The Jewish Passover Festival was near.

[5] When Jesus looked up and saw a great crowd coming toward him, he said to Philip, "Where shall we buy bread for these people to eat?" [6] He asked this only to test him, for he already had in mind what he was going to do.

[7] Philip answered him, "It would take more than half a year's wages to buy enough bread for each one to have a bite!"

[8] Another of his disciples, Andrew, Simon Peter's brother, spoke up, [9] "Here is a boy with five small barley loaves and two small fish, but how far will they go among so many?"

[10] Jesus said, "Have the people sit down." There was plenty of grass in that place, and they sat down (about five thousand men were there). [11] Jesus then took the loaves, gave thanks, and distributed to those who were seated as much as they wanted. He did the same with the fish.

[12] When they had all had enough to eat, he said to his disciples, "Gather the pieces that are left over. Let nothing be wasted." [13] So they gathered them and filled twelve baskets with the pieces of the five barley loaves left over by those who had eaten.

[14] After the people saw the sign Jesus performed, they began to say, "Surely this is the Prophet who is to come into the world."

John 6:1-14

INTRODUCTION
Start Small

As she was preparing to leave, she sighed and said, "It [evangelism] is just so hard." Sara, who works on our church staff, had been discussing evangelism with me in the church office. I think her sigh and statement represent a collective groan from the church when it comes to the area of personal witness. We know it is something we are supposed to do, but it is just so doggone difficult.

The truth is, most sincere Christians truly desire to share the Gospel with the people around them. However, with 62% of us reporting that we have not shared the Gospel in the past six months, desire and action are having trouble meeting.[1] One of the main reasons for this lack of action is because the task feels so overwhelming.

It is overwhelming for two reasons. First, it feels like the people in our lives who are spiritually lost will never get it; their minds are too closed off to the true Jesus. Second, the volume of people who do not know Jesus as their Savior is unfathomably vast. Before long, we fall into the terrible state of I wish I could do everything but because I cannot, I will do nothing. Here is my encouragement and the premise for this book: Start small!

The Jesus Conversation Challenge

Consider how Jesus used a boy's lunch to feed over 5,000 people. It is amazing what God can do when we simply bring what we have to Him. God can do a lot with a little!

This is where it all changed for me. One day I decided, instead of trying to win my whole city, I would simply try to share the Gospel with one person each day. I have come to call it the Jesus Conversation Challenge.

From that first day and first step of faith, I have seen God do more than I could have ever imagined. Sure, I have missed days, but God has been faithful to keep me going and gives me incredible open door opportunities every single day! You will hear lots of stories from these encounters in the pages to come.

Introduction

The goal of this book is to encourage you not to let the difficulty of evangelism keep you from sharing the gospel with the world around you. It is time we start small and commit to doing something. Anyone can bring something to God! Anyone can take a first step of faith. This is precisely the principle I taught my friend Tom when he asked me for help.

"I Need Help"

Tom came to me one day and said, "I want to share my faith with people, but I am scared and have trouble knowing what to say or where to start. I need help. Can I meet with you and learn?" We scheduled a time to meet. We got together in my office for about 15 minutes one day so I could give him some evangelism training.

I shared some advice on how to pray for those far from Jesus and some tips for how to start Gospel conversations. I shared how to push through the fear wave and stay confident when communicating the Gospel. Lastly, I gave Tom my favorite pocket New Testament, with topical help in the front and a salvation plan in the back. I challenged him to give it away that week. Just one. Have one Gospel conversation and give away the Bible.

I am really proud of Tom. He started small. Within the first week, he gave away the New Testament and had a Jesus conversation. That first step turned into a snowball of conversations. In fact, about a year later, he joined the team at Youth for Christ in Cleveland. He told me about dozens of Jesus conversations around high school lunch tables, in gymnasiums, and everywhere in between. God can do a lot with a little!

It was a huge joy to be able to hear him share how he was using some of the evangelism tools at public school lunchrooms and after school clubs. The thing that is exemplary about Tom is not that he took a full time ministry position, but rather that he was willing to ask for help in this critical area. He knew the value of souls and he knew he wanted to share his faith, but he recognized that he needed help.

My friend Tom got off the sidelines and jumped into God's mission for the church. He is a millennial and could have become an evangelism statistic, joining over half the church who have not shared their faith in the past six months. It's too hard, too offensive, too uncomfortable... but instead, Tom identified his weakness and did something about it!

I want to invite you to pull up a chair with Tom. In reality, this book is the expanded version of that first conversation with Tom. I am so excited to share with you the precious truths and tools that God has taught me about evangelism through the years. And, I can't wait for you to

Introduction

hear more stories of God changing people's lives using average people like you and me.

Over the next several pages, we will walk through seven decisions you can make to kickstart a lifestyle of sharing Jesus daily. Each decision leads into the next. At the end of each decision, you will find the "Anyone Can" section which will challenge you to think of ways to put the decision into practice that anyone can do. Let's discover together why it's true that anyone can evangelize!

DECISION #1
Believe

"I have got only one talent: I have no education, but I love the Lord Jesus Christ, and I want to do something for Him." [2]
- **D.L. MOODY**

Decision #1:
I believe God can use me to share the Gospel.

"What, you can't drive?" He looked at me with a matter-of-fact glare. I could barely believe what I was hearing. I was 16 years old and had recently gotten my license. The man I was talking with was the bodyguard for Eminem, the globally renowned hip-hop artist.

Anyone Can Evangelize

At the time, I was working at a place called Pump It Up, which is an inflatable party center for kids. Eminem was hosting his daughter's birthday party there. I had the privilege of being one of the party attendants that worked the party.

I was given a few weeks' notice that I would be working the party and was mentally prepared for meeting Eminem and working his daughter's party. What I did not have time to prepare for was his agent approaching me in the hallway and asking if I would pull Eminem's car around to load in the gifts. Me, drive Eminem's car? I was caught off guard, to say the least.

This opportunity sounded exciting but also terrifying. I questioned his agent, "You want me to drive Eminem's car?" He affirmed and then threw the keys to me. I walked outside and got into the black Escalade. Believe it or not, I made it to the front door with no hiccups. It really was quite a thrill and quite a story, driving Eminem's car.

I believe this is how many of us are with evangelism. We think it sounds exciting to share the Good News of Jesus with another person. We see the need for carrying out the Great Commission, and we have a sense of joy at the idea of being part of someone's salvation. However, fear, hesitation, and insecurity quickly spring up alongside the excitement. We like the idea of evangelism, but actually doing it seems almost impossible.

Decision 1: Believe

I want to normalize this a bit for you. I believe evangelism is intimidating for every Christian. This problem is not specific to you; it is a universal struggle. I remember an interview between Kirk Cameron and Ray Comfort. Ray Comfort has been teaching evangelism for decades and has authored over 80 books.[3] He said, "I am terrified every time I am approaching someone. In fact, every time I sit down on a plane and there is a seat open next to me, I start praying that no one shows up to sit in that seat."[4] I am comforted to know that the "evangelism expert" is terrified just like me and you.

Our faith will play a big factor in whether we succumb to our fears or we conquer them. The more faith we have, the greater our chances of standing up to fear and moving forward. One of my favorite statements in the Bible comes from a father who needed a miracle for his son. Jesus responded to the man's need with the statement, "All things are possible if you believe." The father then said these words to Jesus in Mark 9:24, "I do believe; help my unbelief." That has been a continual prayer of mine: God, give me faith!

The reality is that everything we do in life flows from what we believe. Show me your actions, and I will get a glimpse of your belief system. This is why what we believe is so important. James said it well in James 2:26: "Faith without works is dead." When there are no actions to back up our faith, we are showing that we do not truly believe what we say we do. However, when actions back up our faith, we have a faith that is alive. And when our faith is alive, anything is possible!

The Two Truths We Must Believe

It boils down to two specific truths that we must believe:

Truth #1: Jesus is the only way to Heaven.

Truth #2: I have a part in God's mission, and He has opportunities prepared for me to share the Gospel.

If either one of these two beliefs is not firmly intact, they are like Jenga blocks being pulled out from under us, collapsing our efforts to share our faith. However, when we believe both of these truths wholeheartedly, God can do amazing things through us! Let's break down these two truths a bit further.

Truth #1: Jesus is the only way to Heaven.

First of all, we must believe that Jesus is the only way to heaven. Before this, we must believe that He died for the sins of the world and rose from the dead. His resurrection proves that He is the solution to death—the only solution!

Decision 1: Believe

Jesus' disciples showed that they had this belief firmly intact when they were called in for questioning in front of the religious leaders. Peter and John had just healed a man and were being asked, "By what power or name did you do this?"[5]

Peter responds with some bold and harsh words for the leaders. He states that it is by the name of the One they just finished crucifying. Then, he makes this powerful statement:

> *Salvation is found in no one else, for there is no other name under heaven given to mankind by which we must be saved.* **Acts 4:12**

No one else. We have to be careful that we do not fall for the trap of relativism that says, "This works for me, that works for you, and it is all true." The truth is, Jesus is the only way to heaven.

This is common Christian sense, right? Be on guard. There has been a changing of the winds in several "Christian" circles—and not for the better. These deceptions are both subtle and damaging.

It was in the middle of one of my theology classes at Bible College. I was leaning in with my classmates as we prepared ourselves for a lifetime of service to God. My professor made this striking statement: "The Gospel is anything new."

He was one of a group of professors at this Christian college who were being swept away in a current of progressive views. These universalist views challenged the very Savior they were supposed to be teaching their students about.

The Gospel certainly has the power to make someone new. However, the Christian Gospel could never be reduced to anything new. Our Gospel is very simple. It is the Good News (that's what the Greek word for Gospel means) that Jesus Christ, God's only Son, died on the cross and rose again. Those who trust Him with their lives have eternal life.

Consequently, those who do not believe in Jesus' saving grace are standing in danger of destruction. Have you settled this truth in your heart? If so, this foundational truth will compel you to go into all the world and preach the Gospel!

Truth #2: I have a part in God's mission and He has opportunities prepared for me to share the Gospel.

Second, we must believe there is something we can do to help others come to Jesus, and that God is preparing opportunities for us daily! I had to come to the realization that while I was not going to win the whole world, I do have a part to play. If you consider a good football team, their success is a direct result of all eleven men on the field doing their specific job.

Decision 1: Believe

In the same way, each member of the church needs to do their part if we are going to evangelize the world. No one else is uniquely positioned to be a light for Christ in your workplace, family, neighborhood and social media channels. Overseas mission trips are great, but do not be afraid to start in your neighborhood!

In 2 Corinthians 5:20, Paul says, "We are therefore Christ's ambassadors, as though God were making his appeal through us. We implore you on Christ's behalf: Be reconciled to God." An ambassador is someone who represents and speaks on behalf of another person or country.

As humbling as it is, we are representatives of the Kingdom of God on earth, and we have the privilege of speaking on behalf of Jesus Christ. We are showing our friends and family what Jesus is like. If we stay silent and do not show them love, we essentially say, "Jesus is not interested in you." However, when we invite them in, tell them about God's love, and serve them, we are saying, "Jesus loves you and cares about your life."

It is a huge honor and responsibility to represent Christ. Billy Graham offers this encouragement to us: "The will of God will not take us where the grace of God cannot sustain us."[6] We can be confident that God does indeed have assignments for us and will give us anything we need to complete them well. I remember one of the toughest assignments God has ever given me.

I had lived in my first house for a couple of years when one day after church, I felt God calling me to share the Gospel with every home in my neighborhood. I wish I could tell you I was thrilled at the thought; in reality, I barely believed the thought was from God.

The Spirit would not let this one go, so I made a deal with God—if He sent me a partner, I would obey the call. Sure enough, I met a neighbor not long after who had gotten radically saved out of a lifestyle of darkness and drug use. He shared with me that he was looking for someone to show him the ropes of evangelism.

Shortly after, Tyler (my wingman) and I were off to the races. I had a small map of my neighborhood printed on a piece of paper, and we would highlight in yellow the streets we had completed after we had knocked on each door. This was not the easiest assignment God had given me, but His grace was sufficient. I learned so much through these hundreds of conversations. We were rejected at times, but other people asked questions, prayed with us and heard and understood the Gospel for the first time. God has assignments set up in advance for us, we just have to look for them.

Decision 1: Believe

Here is the reality: There are over 8 billion people in the world, and you and I simply cannot reach them all. In fact, even with a great evangelism partner like Tyler, we cannot even reach 1% of the world's population. Yet, we must do our part to reach the people God puts in our lives. In Matthew 5:14-15, Jesus said these words:

> *You are the light of the world. A city on a hill cannot be hidden. Neither do people light a lamp and put it under a basket. Instead, they set it on a stand, and it gives light to everyone in the house.*

The question is not whether you are a light for Jesus in a dark world; the question is whether or not you have been shining your light. Two things you need to believe if you want to be an effective witness for Jesus: first, that the Gospel is true, and second, that God is preparing opportunities for you! Next, there are a few common excuses that you must overcome so that you will walk through the open doors God gives you.

The Excuses We Must Overcome

As we seek to let the truth of God's Word and God's call sink into our hearts, we can be sure the enemy will try to set traps to keep us from wholehearted acceptance.

The devil especially works to keep Christians from making evangelistic resolutions because this means they are taking ground from him!

The key to winning this battle is to identify the lies and replace them with truth. Dave Ramsey said, "90% of solving a problem is realizing there is one."[7] You may be tempted to accept one of these false mindsets that is hindering your witness without knowing it. So, let's take a look at a few of the most common excuses that keep us from sharing Jesus:

- I don't know enough of the Bible
- I am not bold or outgoing like an evangelist needs to be.
- I will not be able to have any effect on people whose minds are already made up
- I don't have opportunities to share my faith

Excuse #1: I don't know enough of the Bible.

It can be easy to think that we should hide sharing Jesus with people because we do not know enough of the Bible. Fears that we will not be able to answer questions or that we cannot withstand the arguments against Christianity keep us from saying anything about Christ. So, do we let our perceived lack of knowledge keep us from sharing?

Decision 1: Believe

Let's go back to the early church and peek in on one of their first face-offs with the religious leaders. It was a tense moment. The apostles had been preaching and healing in Jesus' name, and the religious leaders were not happy. They arrested Peter and John and brought them in for questioning. Here was their takeaway in Acts 4:13:

> *When they saw the courage of Peter and John and realized that they were unschooled, ordinary men, they were astonished and they took note that these men had been with Jesus.*

Peter and John most likely did not go to school because they were fishermen by trade and certainly did not have religious training. They were ordinary men. The Greek word for "ordinary" is actually the root word for idiot. These were not Bible scholars; they had simply watched and learned from Jesus.

Not every Christian will have the chance to go to Bible college, but we all can watch and learn from Jesus.

Sharkar lived in Bangladesh. Some missionaries came to his village and gave him a copy of the JESUS movie. He became a Christian, and even though he was illiterate, he immediately began sharing his newfound faith. He would tell his Muslim friends, "Did you know the Quran even says that Jesus is coming back one day?" Within weeks, several of his friends had become Christians.

He also started to feel the impact of his decision to follow Jesus. Being a daily wage laborer, he no longer got chosen for jobs. He was beaten, kicked out of his house, and forced to flee from the city he was living in. Within six months, he was forced from home and family, but not before he had won thirty people to Jesus! What a testimony.[8]

Here is a man who had only learned a few months of Christian doctrine. Further, he was illiterate, so he could not even read the Bible. Still, he made connections with his Muslim friends through what he had learned and shared with passion.

From first-century fishermen to Sharkar from Bangladesh, we can see that anyone with a passion for Christ can evangelize. Clearly, theological training and Bible knowledge are not prerequisites for effective evangelism. Simply spend time with Jesus like the first disciples did, and He will teach you everything you need to reach the people around you.

Excuse #2: I am not bold or outgoing like an evangelist needs to be.

To start, we must establish that evangelism is a universal calling for anyone who has begun following Christ. While there is certainly a vocational or ministerial version of the calling of an evangelist as listed in Ephesians 4:11, you

Decision 1: Believe

do not have to be a "full-time" evangelist to share Jesus with your neighbors or family.

Is evangelism something only for a select portion of the church or every member? Again, while I believe some will be more gifted, engage more often, or maybe even be more effective, evangelism is a universal calling.

Think about it this way. When I was born, I was given the last name Stirnemann. Whether I like it or not, everywhere I have gone and will go, I represent that name. Every action and word that I carry out is backed by my last name: Stirnemann.

When you are born again, you take on Jesus' name. You are part of His family. Thus, every action and word represent Him. You immediately become the example of Christ to the world around you. If you think about it, you are evangelizing to everyone in your life, whether you like it or not.

Let's recall Jesus' words from Matthew 5:14, "You are the light of the world, a city on a hill cannot be hidden." The light of the world is your identity as a believer. You cannot be hidden. A light always sticks out in the dark. The Great Commission is a universal command. Do not avoid it; simply embrace it. You are the light of the world.

The key is to shine in your own way. My wife and I could not be more different. I am outgoing and love adventure.

Anyone Can Evangelize

My wife is meek and prefers spending time at home. If anyone could use the excuse that evangelism is not their natural gifting, it would be my wife. She is task-oriented, detailed, and a woman of few words.

She has gifts, but going up to people to talk about Jesus would not be her natural modus operandi. Evangelism comes fairly naturally to me. It is still a discipline because my flesh reverts to talking about football instead of faith. Still, just based on personality, I would probably have ten times the Jesus conversations my wife would have in any given year.

However, this is a big however, Rachel still chooses to share Christ. I have been amazed to watch her invite her family members to church, pray for them, and talk about what God has done in her life. I remember arriving home one day as she was talking about Jesus with the internet installation worker.

At one point, we purchased a few hundred sunflower seed packets and had the words "Seeds of Hope: Jesus loves you" printed on the back. Rachel would give them to people when she was out and about. Thus, in her own way, she has chosen to shine her light.

No, she is not on the church's evangelism team. She is usually clicking the slides at the computer. When she

Decision 1: Believe

has the opportunity, she tries to share the Gospel with those around her. I am proud of her for saying "yes" to the Great Commission. I think she is a great example of how, no matter your personality type, God has called all of us to evangelize.

Excuse #3: I will not be able to have any effect on people whose minds are already made up.

Evangelism can feel like an impossible task. Many people start out sharing their faith when they are first saved. Then, after a few unsuccessful attempts, they become discouraged and eventually give up altogether. In 2 Corinthians 4:4, we learn what we are up against when it comes to trying to convert people to Christ: "The god of this age has blinded the minds of unbelievers, so that they cannot see the light of the gospel that displays the glory of Christ, who is the image of God."

Prayer is the most important factor in opening people's minds to the Gospel, which, by the way, is something anyone can do! We will talk in-depth on praying for the lost in the next chapter. With such a strong opposition from so many, is there any point for us to try to share our faith? There are thousands upon thousands of testimonies of hard hearts being softened by God. In fact, all of our hearts were there at one point, and most of the time,

Anyone Can Evangelize

He uses someone to share the Gospel along the way. Here is one such story:

He was a retired doctor. Quite possibly, he was the most negative person I had ever had a conversation with. He had recently lost his wife and was grieving. Everything we discussed, he saw the negative in the situation or topic. For him, the glass was not just half empty; it was completely empty! When the topic of religion came up, he quickly quoted Karl Marx, stating that religion is the "opiate of the masses."

After meeting my new friend, I was immediately burdened for his salvation. I spent the next two years praying for him whenever I thought of him and checking in on his grief journey occasionally. At one point, about a year after we had met, I took the time to share the Gospel with him. I explained about the grace that Jesus offers and the hope that comes with a relationship with Him. It did not seem to make a big difference, but he did listen to what I had to say.

The last time I talked to him, he said that he was dating someone. I said I was happy to hear about the new relationship. He stated that he was going to church with her. I was intrigued. He went on to say that he was very much enjoying the sermon, and he had come to the conclusion that he believed in God! I could barely believe my ears! I

Decision 1: Believe

never heard if he had made a profession of faith in Christ, but he was certainly heading in that direction. It is amazing what God can do with our small efforts.

Even though people can be stubborn and their hearts can be hard, it is important that we stay focused on God. He is able to reach even the worst sinner with His grace. Do not call impossible what God calls possible. Here is a simple Scripture to help you overcome the excuse that people are too far from God for you to even try: Isaiah 59:1a, "Surely the arm of the LORD is not too short to save." Do not lie to yourself that God cannot reach someone. After all, He reached you and I! He is able to save; and you are able to evangelize.

Excuse #4: I don't have opportunities to share my faith.

Recently I was at my church life group, when Jeannine, one of the members of our group, shared about a rare medical issue she was up against. The eye doctor was planning to perform a routine surgery to help with some scar tissue behind her eye when he discovered that her retina had become detached from her eye. After surgery, the doctor had to create pressure to keep the retina reattached. As a result, Jeannine had to keep her head down for 45 minutes out of each hour for an entire week.

Anyone Can Evangelize

She shared how difficult her life was, having to keep her head down. She described the sheer joy she experienced being able to look up and see out the window or look into the eyes of the family members or friends that she was spending time with. Her head had been forced face downward 75% of her waking hours.

It made me think about how many Christians are walking around with their heads down. They have plenty of opportunities around them to shine the light of Christ to their community, but their heads are down. They are too distracted and discouraged to see the opportunities in front of them. Jesus said it this way in John 4:35: "Do you not say, 'There are yet four months and then comes the harvest?' Look up, I tell you, the fields are white with harvest."

One of my friends at church, named Dwayne, said it this way: "I do not think the issue is that Christians today do not have opportunities to share their faith; it is that they are not looking for them." It is a sobering thought to think that people whose eternities are in jeopardy are walking by us, and we are missing the opportunities to share the hope of Christ with them.

The British preacher and author Leonard Ravenhill, puts his finger on the root of the problem: "We are too busy with the dust of time in our eyes to get the tears of eternity moving." Is that our condition? Are we too busy

Decision 1: Believe

building our kingdom when we have neglected God's Kingdom? The Scripture clearly shows us that God is preparing good works for us to do. Further, God has gifted us and blessed us with His Holy Spirit. Are we stewarding the gifts of salvation and the Holy Spirit well?

A few months ago, my son gave me a much-needed wake-up call. Caleb and I had just finished visiting a house that was decked out with Christmas lights and were headed home. As we made a left turn, a piece of someone's bumper that had fallen in the road got caught under our van. I was forced to pull over. I realized what had happened. The man whose car had been in an accident was parked just a few feet behind me. I walked over to him and his car with the piece of bumper in my hand.

After talking for a moment, I saw that the other car was parked at a kitty corner across the intersection, and the police officer was on his way. I allowed myself to become irritated at the delay, tossed the piece of bumper toward the man's vehicle, and told him I hoped everything worked out. As I was getting back to the car with Caleb, he looked at me and said, "Don't you think we should tell him about Jesus?" Suddenly, I realized my selfishness and error.

I spun around and took a few moments to show genuine concern for the man's situation. Then I asked if he knew the Lord. He said that he knew about Christ but was not living for Him. I explained that this would be a great time for the man to use the interruption in his life to turn his life to Christ. He allowed me to pray for him, and Caleb and I headed for home.

My 7-year-old son helped me not miss the opportunity right in front of me. My head had been down until God used Caleb to open my eyes. He said, "Look up, Dad!" It made me reflect on the whole situation. Why had the bumper lodged under my car? Why had I pulled directly in front of this man? And why did I have a window of time with no one but him and I at his damaged car? Could it be that God was setting me up? And the man in the wreck?! I am very thankful that, thanks to Caleb, I was able to make the most of the opportunity.

Make a commitment to step into the opportunities God gives to you. He tests us to see if our minds are focused on eternal or earthly matters. If we are stuck in earthly thinking, we will convince ourselves that we have no evangelistic opportunities. But when we look for God's divine appointments, we are ready to be used by Him. It all starts with believing that He can use you!

It is time for you to dismantle the excuses in your life that discourage you from evangelizing. Replacing lies with truth accomplishes two things. First, it encourages our spirit to do what is right. Truthful thinking aligns us with

Decision 1: Believe

God's will—His will for us to help people see His Son. Second, it forces the enemy to flee. Lying is the only language that Satan knows.

When we cast out excuses and meditate on truth, our ship has left the devil's port. Jesus said, "The truth will set you free." Part of our Christian freedom is the privilege of sharing with others the life we have found in Jesus!

Lord, Send Me

What an opportunity we have in this moment of darkness! As I walk through malls or movie theaters, I see a depth of lostness in people I have never witnessed before. There is hopelessness in their eyes that brings me to tears. It is as if they are silently asking if there is any hope or meaning to life, having found only "no" for an answer. Yet, here we stand at the door of opportunity.

Did you know that 44% of U.S. adults described themselves as more open to God today than before the pandemic? Even more striking, 75% reported that they have a desire to grow spiritually.[9] People are

> **Did you know that 44% of U.S. adults described themselves as 'more open to God today than before the pandemic'? Even more striking, 75% reported that they 'have a desire to grow spiritually'.**

searching for God. Churches around the United States and beyond are seeing a tremendous influx of visitors. With all this in mind, Christ-followers face a crossroads. Will we push through our excuses and offer God's grace to those who are spiritually lost? The choice is ours.

The prophet Isaiah faced a similar situation to ours today. At the end of Isaiah 5, we find this description of the culture, "And if one looks at the land, there is only darkness and distress; even the sun will be darkened by clouds. (Isaiah 5:30b)" Only darkness.

Then, in Isaiah 6, God dramatically calls Isaiah. He asks in Isaiah 6:8, "Whom shall I send? And who will go for us?" A moment of silence follows, as if all of heaven and earth wait to see if anyone will answer. Then Isaiah says five words that have the power to change the world, "Here I am. Send me!"

God is looking for others to send into this dark world with the light of the Gospel. Millions of people held captive by darkness are waiting for your answer to God's call: "Will you go for Me?"

This is where faith comes in. Will you believe that Jesus has the power to save anyone, anywhere? And will you choose to believe that He not only can use you, but has assignments with your name on them? If faith is rising in your heart, it is time to respond with Isaiah: "Here I am. Send me."

Jesus Burgers

A willing Christian is one that is useful to God. A group of college students from California proved this. Isla Vista is a college party town right next to the University of California, Santa Barbara. A few college students armed with the love of Jesus and a grill started giving away burgers to the college students lining the streets at house parties.

From that first night in 2001, over one hundred thousand Jesus Burgers have been given away! The ministry now owns a house on one of the busiest party streets in town. They lead times of worship, pray over students and have seen thousands of students touched by the Gospel since the ministry began.[10] So, if you can flip a burger and say a prayer, you might just be an evangelist!

Being a part of God's redemption story in someone's life will be better than anything you could imagine. As God has used me in small ways to bring people to Himself, I have found a joy that I cannot describe. I want to invite you to join me in this adventure.

You don't need all your ducks in a row, you just need some faith. Belief precedes action. If we truly believe Jesus is the only way to heaven, it will spark a passion in us to share that with others. If we believe God's Word which tells us that we are His ambassadors and He has preordained opportunities for us to share His Gospel, we will live with a different mindset.

Start each day expecting that God will give you opportunities to share the Gospel. Have a mindset that He can and will use you. Believe it. Make it your habit to start every day with the prayer: "Lord, send me!" That's a prayer anyone can pray. As we venture into our second decision, we come to potentially the most important aspect of evangelism: prayer.

Anyone Can...

The Anyone Can section will conclude each chapter's decision. The idea is simple, in order to put the decision into action, you are going to take a step. The concept of anyone can is based on two incredible stories. The first is the loaves and fish story from the Bible.

Jesus used a boy's small lunch (and the disciples' obedience in bringing it to Him) to feed over 5,000 people. This story proves that all it takes is a small step of faith from us for God to do a miracle. Early in adulthood and ministry,

Decision 1: Believe

I used to swing for the fences. Now, I tell myself almost daily: start small. "Do not despise small beginnings, the Lord rejoices to see the work begin." (See Zechariah 4:10). Bring what you have and watch what God can do.

The second is Kendra Adachi's story that she shares in her groundbreaking book entitled The Lazy Genius. Her book covers lots of ways to be a 'lazy genius', but I would like to highlight only one. Adachi argues that many people fail because their resolutions and goals are too grandiose.

For example, the person looking to get in shape makes an eating plan, five day per week workout plan and tries to overhaul their lifestyle with dramatic changes. Acachi teaches to start small, really small. She shares how she began her workout shift with one down dog pose per day, and things took off from there.[11]

I have tried this approach with many areas of my life and I have been amazed at how incredibly it works. So, grab your journal or your small group and come up with a few ways you can turn our first decision into action that anyone can do. I will give you one per chapter as a starting point:

DECISION #1:

I believe God can use me to share the Gospel

Anyone Can:
Anyone can memorize Romans 1:16, "For I am not ashamed of the gospel, because it is the power of God that brings salvation to everyone who believes: first to the Jew, then to the Gentile."

Further reading:
Anyone But Me by Ray Comfort
Just As I Am by Billy Graham

For your playlist:
Send Me by River Valley Worship

DECISION #2
Pray

"There are 3 factors to a successful evangelistic crusade - prayer, prayer, and prayer!" [12]
- BILLY GRAHAM

Decision #2:
I will pray for the lost daily.

Teen Challenge and Life Challenge drug and alcohol rehabilitation centers operate in over 1,400 centers across 129 nations.[13] Each center takes in young people trapped in addiction and uses Biblical discipleship to help them restore their lives. I have several friends who have found freedom through their ministry. Studies show that 70% of their graduates stay sober and addiction free![14] While their ministry is remarkable, it is the backstory of Teen Challenge's founding that I want to share with you.

The year was 1958, and David Wilkerson had been pastoring a church in Philipsburg, Pennsylvania for just over a year. After busy days of ministry and life with a newborn daughter, Wilkerson had developed a habit of watching TV for two hours each evening after his wife and family went to bed. He enjoyed watching the late show.

One night, he had an idea: *What if I traded watching TV for two hours for praying for two hours to end my day?* While pondering the idea, he was keenly aware that part of him did NOT like this proposition! That night, he struck a deal with God.

He decided to list his TV for sale in the paper. If someone called to buy it within 30 minutes of the newspaper ad hitting the street, he would know this new habit was something he needed to pursue. At the 29-minute mark after the ad appeared, he was getting ready to breathe a sigh of relief and think about what to watch that evening when his phone rang. The caller stated they were coming immediately to buy the TV. Just like that, the TV was gone and his evening prayer challenge began.

He faithfully spent two hours in prayer each evening for a few months. During one of these prayer times, he saw

Decision 2: Pray

a sketch of the Puerto Rican gang members who were on trial for murder in a *Life Magazine* on his desk. At first, he dismissed the magazine article and picture as a distraction from prayer! But then, as he began to cry and feel his heart break for these youth, he realized that this was God at work in him. A thought came seemingly from out of nowhere: *Go to New York and help those boys.*

From there, he made his way to New York City and from that prayer time, the first Teen Challenge was planted in NYC. Since then, hundreds of youth and their families have been impacted for Christ by this crazy act of faith! I will share more of how he connected with the gang members in chapter four, but for now, let's focus on his example of prayer. [15]

Here is the point that I do not want you to miss: There was a sacrifice before there was a breakthrough. There was a great cost to the incredible miracles. If Wilkerson had decided he enjoyed his TV too much after God stirred his heart, would God have sent someone else to NYC? Or would this region have remained unchanged and Teen Challenge never begun? What people, regions and ministries in our lives remain untouched by the power of God because we are too pre-

> **There was a sacrifice before there was a breakthrough.**

occupied with lesser things to give ourselves to prayer and His purposes?!

David Wilkerson's story has been a catalyst for much of my own passion for prayer and for the lost in my life. Of course, he was not perfect. He was a human just like you and me. But something of his example and passion have moved my heart and broken me through the years. In fact, about five years ago, I tried my own version of his TV deal.

I told God I wanted to get serious about how I was spending my time in the evening, and I did not want to waste it when I could use it to build His Kingdom. Just after having this conversation with God, a family member was at my house. She looked at my nice big TV and said, "I like that TV. I would like to have it if you are looking to get rid of it." *What in the world I thought? Don't touch my TV.* But, of course, I remembered my prayer and gave the television to her!

I have not been faithful to praying two hours per night for five years, but I have found a sweetness in my evening prayer times that is indescribable. While morning devotions can center us on Christ and prepare us to be in alignment with Him for the day, the evening has a different power.

We are tired, sometimes having loose ends or open frustrations. Taking these to God instead of going first to our usual show or ice cream has a way of developing a deep

Decision 2: Pray

intimacy with and dependence on Christ. Where do you run when you are weary?

Sacrifice and Calling

Prayer can create dynamic power in our personal witness. It is truly the ignition of the motor of evangelism! Two things I want to highlight about Wilkerson's story before we dive into some practical tips for praying for the unsaved:

1) He started with a big sacrifice.

2) Prayer opened the door to his calling.

First, prayer is *always a sacrifice*. There are always a million other things we could be doing with our time. Anytime you bow your head or take to your knees, you are choosing to be dependent on God instead of something else. That is where the power is! Listen to Paul's words in Romans 12:1: "Offer your bodies as a living sacrifice, holy and pleasing to God."

Some people act as if New Testament believers do not need to sacrifice anymore. Sure, we do not have to kill any more animals. And yes, Jesus was the final sacrifice for our sins. However, we are called to lay down our lives in order to make room for Jesus and His Spirit to take the main seat in our lives! You and I have to get onto the altar and offer ourselves to God if we want to be used by Him.

One of my concerns is that many Christians try to start right into evangelism without a prayer life to sustain them. They may start out on fire and try to tell people about Jesus (which is wonderful!) but their personal prayer life is not strong enough to withstand the disinterest, tension, or rejection that comes with witnessing. Leonard Ravenhill said these striking words:

> "Prayer is not preparation for the battle; prayer is the battle."[16]

We win in the place of prayer. Our prayer life is where we gain a deep love for God. We bear our burden for the people we are praying for to be saved, and we become resolute in our stance to stay with God and His mission no matter what we face. Coming out of this place, discussing Jesus with others can flow out of us.

Second, the secret place with God is where we develop our anointing for our calling. Even though he did not know it, it was those late evenings in prayer that God was using to prepare David Wilkerson to win the New York gang members to Christ and launch a worldwide ministry. In fact, it is where He gave him a specific vision and word for where to go. What sacrifice do you need to make to prepare yourself for what God is calling you to do?

Decision 2: Pray

Ten Secrets to Praying Effectively for the Lost

Our next step is to get a Biblical basis for how to pray for those who don't yet believe. Manley Beasley said this about the topic: "Praying for the lost is an area about which much is said but little is known or understood." I agree with his statement, but I say, let's go get some knowledge and understanding! There are so many victories ready to be won by any believer who steps into the realm of praying for the lost!

Over the next few pages, I am going to offer 10 secrets to praying effectively for the lost. I still have so much to learn in this area, but these are some things that either the Lord has taught me or believers who went before us have helped me to understand. I will give a Scripture with each secret and some help as you put it into practice.

Secret #1: Simply Ask

This is the confidence we have in approaching God: that if we ask anything according to his will, he hears us. And if we know that he hears us—whatever we ask—we know that we have what we asked of him.
1 John 5:14-15

All we have to do is ask. Let's not overcomplicate this. If one of my kids wants a cookie, their starting point is simply asking for the cookie. They do not need to start by telling me how good the cookie is, why they deserve it, or why it fits into their diet. They just need to start by asking. Scriptures like 1 John 5:14-15 gives us confidence in our praying because it says if the request is according to God's will, we have what we asked for.

The good news is, salvation of souls is absolutely according to God's will. It is His desire that none should perish (2 Peter 3:9). Further, Jesus already died for their sins. Their forgiveness is already available; they just need to agree with His grace. Your prayer is helping to align their life with what Jesus has already done for them. So start by simply asking for them to be saved!

Secret #2: Go to War

> *The weapons we fight with are not the weapons of the world. On the contrary, they have divine power to demolish strongholds.* **2 Corinthians 10:4**

Many Christians comment on the great difficulty of evangelism. This verse gives us the reason it is so difficult: it is a war. Not only does the Scripture say that the lost are under the strong man's control, but they are also children of the devil (John 8:44), blinded to the Gospel (2 Corinthians 4:3-4), and lie under the power of the evil one (1 John 5:19). In fact, Isaiah 14:17 states that the

Decision 2: Pray

devil keeps people as prisoners of war. Thus, we have to get some force in our prayers and take what the enemy has stolen.

The weapons that we have are strong enough to win this war. Remember, greater is He who is in you than he who is in the world (1 John 4:4). We have also been given armor for these battles. Often, when I pray for the lost, I will recite the pieces of armor found in Ephesians 6:10-18. Then I do my best to go to war.

Recently, someone told me the story of a group of Christians who were praying for a persecuted Christ follower who was in jail. There was commotion in the prison that kept the believer from sleeping except for one hour every night.

When the man was released, he shared with the church about the one hour of quiet sleep he received each night. It was found to be the exact same hour that the church met every evening to pray for him. Do not be discouraged; God is moving when you are praying. Don't be naïve; there is a battle. And the victory belongs to praying believers!

Secret #3: Pray Through

About midnight Paul and Silas were praying and singing hymns to God, and the other prisoners were listening to them. Suddenly there was such a violent earth-

quake that the foundations of the prison were shaken. At once all the prison doors flew open, and everyone's chains came loose. **Acts 16:25-26**

Someone from my church shared a very interesting note from a former Satanist (turned Christian) who was teaching on the topic of prayer. He stated that Satanists have an advantage in prayer because they often gather and stay up praying to Satan all night, while Christians often pray for something for ten minutes and then move on.

We need to discern when endurance and persistence are needed. Jesus often prayed all night. The persistent widow prayed until she got her answer. Jesus is still asking us today, "Will I find such faith on the earth when I return?"

You must be willing to pray until the prison doors break open. Praying through is the idea of praying until there is a strong sense that the battle has been won. One mother reported that she knew her son would be saved because she felt a breakthrough of peace in the spiritual realm while she was interceding for him. Sure enough, within a short amount of time, he was free from the drugs and the wild lifestyle he was living and had submitted his life to Christ![17] When you have a burden for someone, pray until it passes, and watch what God will do!

Decision 2: Pray

Secret #4: Never Give Up

> *And will not God bring about justice for his chosen ones, who cry out to him day and night? Will he keep putting them off? I tell you, he will see that they get justice, and quickly. However, when the Son of Man comes, will he find faith on the earth?* **Luke 18:7-8**

A good friend of mine had to pray for thirteen years to see his extended family return to Christ. For those thirteen years, he did not see much change. Then, the floodgates opened and thirteen of his family members were at church with him on a Sunday morning. I had the privilege of seeing four of them baptized at our Good Friday service this past year!

The difference between our previous secret and this one is that praying through is in regard to a specific time of prayer. When we sit down to pray, there are times we have an assignment in prayer to intercede for. We need to discern those times and pray until the burden lifts. Then, there is the secret we come to now in which we commit to not giving up. This is the principle of believing in God for something even if it takes weeks, months, years or a lifetime of praying in the same direction.

George Muller, famous missionary to England, committed to pray for five of his unsaved friends every day. Three of them were saved within the first eleven years of his prayers, but two remained unsaved even until Muller's death.

When he had been asked about these men who were still unsaved, he said, "How could they not be saved? I am praying for them." Altogether, he prayed for them for 52 years. Within a few months of his passing, the final two were both saved! Do not give up! What friend do you need to commit to praying for daily?[18]

Secret #5: Ask for Open Doors

And pray for us, too, that God may open a door for our message, so that we may proclaim the mystery of Christ, for which I am in chains. **Colossians 4:3**

I will never forget one of the first times I prayed this prayer. I was a senior in high school, and I asked God for open doors to share Christ as I walked into school that day. Later at lunch, a friend of mine asked me about my church. He asked what the Pastor talked about when he preached. This friend had never shown interest in faith conversations before. Ask God for opportunities and he will give them to you!

A few months back, I prayed a rather unique prayer one morning. I said, "God, I am feeling a bit lazy today. Can you send someone to my doorstep for me to share the Gospel with?"

Decision 2: Pray

As I was returning home from a late-night walk, a man walking his two dogs crossed my path just as I arrived at my driveway. We began chatting. He said that he had recently seen a sign on the side of the road that said you have to be born again. He then asked me what that meant. I was able to share with him what it means to be born again.

It was not until I walked through my door that I remembered my prayer for someone to come to my doorstep. God sure did answer that one! He must really want people to be saved! So, if you have lacked opportunities to share... just ask for them!

Secret #6: Pray for Workers

> *Then He said to His disciples, "The harvest is plentiful, but the workers are few. Ask the Lord of the harvest, therefore, to send out workers into His harvest."*
> **Matthew 9:37-38**

Jesus made it clear, there are a lot of people ready to come to Christ! The harvest is large, but there is a lack of harvesters. So, we pray for God to send out witnesses.

Pray for God to send out workers both at home and overseas. In places such as Afghanistan, only 2.9% of the non-Christians are personally acquainted with a Christian.[19] Workers are needed all over the world.

Ask God to send workers to the unsaved people in your own life whom you have been praying for. While we ask God to send out others, we must raise our own hand as well and pray, "God, send me today."

Secret #7: Ask for the Nations

Ask me, and I will make the nations your inheritance, the ends of the earth your possession. **Psalm 2:8**

Sometimes, we pray too small. Imagine you have a dad who is a lawyer... and a doctor! You are heading to the mall and you say, "Dad, is there any way I could have $4, maybe $5 if you can afford it?" How ridiculous! If you are smart, you will ask that dad for $300 for your mall trip.

The same is true of our God. He owns the world, and He instructs us to ask Him for the nations as our inheritance! So, while we certainly want to pray with diligence for individuals to be saved, let's also ask God for the nations.

Secret #8: Fasting

However, this kind does not go out except by prayer and fasting. **Mark 9:29 NKJV**

One of the best and most effective ways to see God answer our prayers for the unsaved is to team our prayers with fasting. There are occasions all through Scripture where God moved in powerful ways through fasting.

Decision 2: Pray

Daniel kept himself from being drawn into the hypnosis of Babylon by praying and fasting. Esther saved the whole nation of Israel by calling for a fast.

Further, Jesus told us in Luke 5:35, "...when the bridegroom will be taken from them; in those days they will fast." What did He mean? He meant that as soon as He left the earth, His followers would be fasting to keep His power and presence close to them. He did not say they might fast, He said they will fast. Have you been obeying Jesus on this front?

If you have not taken up the challenge of establishing a fasting routine, I would ask you to consider doing so before God. Ever since I took up a weekly meal to fast and pray, I have had greater peace, greater victory, and a place to engage in the greatest battles I am called to fight. I believe some of the people in our lives will only come to Christ if we pray and fast for them.

A young man put on his headphones during the worship time and I was mad. It was Sunday morning, and Hayden, a teenager at my church, was checked out. I was about to go up and say something when I restrained myself and decided to take a different approach.

I keep a prayer and fasting space open each week for whatever big request comes my way. I took on praying for

Hayden. Not only that, but I took him out for a smoothie and to run an errand with me. That was it—love and some prayer and fasting. Anyone can do what I did.

It was God's turn. Nearly a year after I had spent time with Hayden, he came up to me for prayer after a Sunday morning message. He told me that he had taken an evening to pray and the "Holy Spirit showed up."

Now, he wanted his girlfriend to experience God like he had and was wondering if I would pray with him for her to know God. Both were baptized this past summer! Truth be told, they both still have a lot of growing up to do. Maybe it's time for someone to pray and fast for them again!

Fast and pray, and watch God work miracles.

Secret #9: Pray with Friends

> *Again, truly I tell you that if two of you on earth agree about anything they ask for, it will be done for them by my Father in heaven.* **Matthew 18:19**

Praying alone for the unsaved is good; praying with others for the unsaved is better. There is power and encouragement in numbers. It is a spiritual principle that our fruitfulness multiplies when we have more than one. Jesus sent out his disciples in twos, and the first mission-

Decision 2: Pray

ary journeys in Acts were done in twos. The "Bible math" in Deuteronomy 32:30 states that when God is involved, one can take on one thousand but two can defeat ten thousand! If you can get more than two praying for someone's salvation, even better!

Recently, the young adult leadership team at our church got together and prayed for the salvation of two young men who we knew had been coming to the church but had not yet made a profession of faith. We took about ten minutes to intercede for the two of them. Within two weeks, both had made a commitment to Jesus! One came directly to me asking how to start his relationship with God, and the other responded to a salvation altar call. There is power when Christians come together in agreement.

If your church does not have a small group focused on praying for the lost, consider starting one. If you are married, begin praying with your spouse for your children and family members' salvations. My wife and I set aside Thursday nights for these prayers.

Get creative in establishing the practice of praying with friends, finding others to intercede for lost souls alongside you. The enemy does not easily give up on people that belong to him, so we need to join forces to win these important battles!

Secret #10: Let the Spirit Lead

In the same way, the Spirit helps us in our weakness. We do not know what we ought to pray for, but the Spirit himself intercedes for us through wordless groans.
Romans 8:26

Each person and situation is unique. The Holy Spirit knows what needs to happen for them to come to Him. When we take time to ask the Holy Spirit for guidance, we can see what stronghold is hindering someone from putting their faith in Jesus.

For two years, I had been committed to praying for neighbor David's salvation. I specifically prayed for him almost every day. One day, while I was mowing the grass, a powerful burden came over me to pray for David. It was so strong that I got on my knees right in my front yard and began praying. Almost immediately, the Holy Spirit spoke to me, "Do not pray for his salvation, he is a lost son."

I stood up and began meditating on the words I had just heard. I changed my prayers from that point and began asking God to bring the prodigal home. Almost immediately, I saw a change in him. First, he mentioned visiting church again with his parents. He appeared happier and more lighthearted. We were able to talk more openly, even about faith, which he had avoided before.

Decision 2: Pray

A few months after I had moved away from the neighborhood, I received a text from David. It read, "So, I did a thing today!" It was a picture of him getting baptized that Sunday at his church. My eyes welled up with tears as I knew God had answered my prayer for this lost son to be found again. Since then, he has continued to text my wife and me about his growing faith in God, his church involvement, and finding a girlfriend who also loves Christ! To God be the glory!

The Power of Prayer

Pastor Lee Thomas, author of the powerful book Praying Effectively for the Lost, shares the story of a pastor named Wayne who experienced an incredible breakthrough in prayer:

> Wayne has a God-given burden for inmates on death-row and spends much time in the prisons trying to win them to Christ. He continues his story: "A major victory involves a death-row inmate recently executed at the prison in Huntsville, Texas. He was a very dedicated Muslim; morally better than most Christians I know. I had been working with him for about two years, sharing the gospel with him and having my church pray for him - all in vain. He would write to me, ending his letters with, 'Allah be with you.' I

never felt more hopeless or helpless over any case. Then, about two months before his execution date in September 2002, I encouraged our church to pray specifically to bind the strong man of False Religion and to plead the blood of Christ over him. Instantly a change began to take place. He began to admit that Jesus was a good teacher, and his letters now ended with 'God be with you.' He invited me to be present at his execution. I made the trip to Huntsville to see him one last time. How my heart was thrilled when he asked me, 'What must I do to trust Christ for salvation?' At 3:05 p.m. he asked the Lord Jesus to save him. Fifty-one hours and twelve minutes later he was dead. Just two hours before his execution he winked at me and said, 'I love you and I'll be waiting for you in heaven. And the very last words he spoke on earth were these:' God forgives. He's the greatest!" He died with such a peaceful look on his face that even the warden commented on it.[20]

The Pastor and church had prayed for *two years* without success! Then, they got their prayer directed at the right target. There are no formulas in prayer, but the Holy Spirit will guide us. When He does, follow and pray what He reveals. Thanks to this faithful church in Texas, that man is in heaven today.

Decision 2: Pray

There are many more keys to praying for the lost. The depths of prayer are as endless as the God we pray to. The crucial point is to establish a habit in your life of setting aside time every day to pray for lost people.

Ever since I committed to pray for the lost daily, the Holy Spirit will not let me fall asleep until I spend at least a moment on my knees by my bedside praying for one lost person. I am grateful for a God who cares so deeply for those who are far from Him.

Before you rush out to evangelize, pray! Enter into the powerful cycle of praying and preaching. Knees, feet, knees, feet, repeat! Our prayer life will sustain our evangelistic efforts. Anyone can evangelize, and anyone can pray. We now turn our attention to the best motivation from which we share Jesus with people: love.

DECISION #2:

I will pray for the lost daily.

Grab your journal or your small group and come up with a few ways you can turn our second decision into action that anyone can do. Here is one for a starting point for our second decision:

Anyone Can:
Take two minutes per day to intercede for a lost person.

Further reading:
Praying Effectively for the Lost by Lee E. Thomas
The Cross and the Switchblade
by David Wilkerson
Why Revival Tarries by Leonard Ravenhill

For your playlist:
Tears of the Saints by Leeland

DECISION #3

Love

"You already love your heavenly Father, and you know that this stranger is created by Him, but separated from Him, so take those first steps in evangelism because you love God." [21]
- JOHN PIPER

Decision #3:
I will establish love as the reason for my evangelism.

One day my friend Tyler and I were at the mall sharing our faith with the people that we met. We began talking with a young adult about faith in Christ. He was a tough sell! When it was clear that the conversation was going nowhere fast, I decided to share with him why we were out witnessing. I explained that we cared about him. We cared about his future and his soul. We believed Jesus was the only way to heaven and we wanted heaven to be his future, not the alternative! It was striking to watch this young man's disposition change.

When we first started talking with him, he was defensive and argumentative. He was ready to defend his indifference to the things of Christ. But when we showed our love for him, he sensed that we genuinely cared. When he realized we were not there to force our ideology down his throat, his countenance changed. If we cannot reach people with our eloquent arguments, let's reach them with our love!

Love is the best motivation for our evangelism. Zach Williams, one of my favorite music artists, has a song titled *Heart of God*. The chorus's main line says, "There's only love in the heart of God." I love that line. That needs to be our aim for what fills our hearts as well. Yet, through our days and lives, many other motives and hindrances lodge in our hearts. Removing these opens the door to God's love, leading to a more fruitful life. Before we explore how to center our hearts on love, let's examine what we need to remove.

Decision 3: Love

Heart Detox

Selfish Ambition

Do nothing out of selfish ambition or vain conceit. Rather, in humility value others above yourselves, not looking to your own interests but each of you to the interests of the others. **Philippians 2:3-4**

Selfish ambition runs rampant in our world today. It always has, but now, King Self has never been more fashionable. A quick trip through social media shows not only selfish ambition but advertisements seducing you to build your own kingdom.

Allowing Self to sit on the throne of our hearts leads to one of two outcomes. Either we ignore the work of evangelism because we do not "feel like it," or we do it with an eye on self-glorification instead of God's glory.

John "Praying" Hyde, a missionary in the late 1800s, tells this story. At one point in his ministry, God was allowing him to see four souls saved per day! On days when the four souls had not come in, he would pray and ask God what was misaligned. Hyde confessed that most often, it was a "want of praise." He said he would ask God for a spirit of praise, and after focusing his worship on God, the remaining souls would come in for that day![22]

Who have you been praising? It is so easy to subtly begin worshiping ourselves, even within the church. Ambition is good, selfish ambition is not. One thing God does not share is His glory. Do whatever it takes to eliminate selfish ambition from your life. Souls depend on it.

Fear

There is no fear in love, but perfect love casts out fear.
1 John 4:18

Possibly no emotion is more difficult to overcome than fear, especially in evangelism! Ray Comfort offers this illustration to help us with our fears of witnessing. Suppose you are at a pool party with your friends. You keep walking to the edge of the water and dip your toe in, but because it feels too cold, you stay on the side.

Hours pass, and you continue waiting, not wanting to get cold, talking to your friends in your chair. Then suddenly a child walking on the edge falls in and begins to drown. You do not think—you dive straight in, and pull the child to the surface.[23]

It is the same in evangelism. In view of eternity, love compels us to jump in. Perfect love for the lost can cast out our fears and reservations. Ask God to fill you with His perfect love.

Decision 3: Love

John Maxwell shares valuable advice he received about facing fears. Maxwell attended a seminar at the University of Dayton in which W. Clement Stone spoke on the topic of having a sense of urgency. This simple practice was Maxwell's big takeaway from Stone's teaching:

> Before bed, sit on the edge of your bed and say "do it now" 40 times. Then, when you wake up, before you do anything else, sit up and say "do it now" 40 times. Here is what will begin to happen: When faced with something that you know you need to do but fear creeps in, your mind will automatically think, "do it now" and you will be able to push through the fear and act with courage.[24]

Do not put up with fear any longer. Fear is a liar. Do it now. Decide that the love in your heart will be stronger than the fear. Fear can be persistent—keep working at it. You will lose sometimes, but do not give up. Love requires an enduring spirit. For further help in this area, read *Breaking Intimidation* by John Bevere.

Finally, understand that fear is something that can be cast out. I am not talking about the fear of running into the middle of traffic. That is a good fear. But when we are paralyzed while trying to do things we know God has called us to do, we must take authority over our fears.

In 2 Timothy 1:7, Paul writes, "God did not give us a spirit of fear but power, love and soundness of mind." Realize that you are dealing with a spirit, and it is NOT from God. So cast it out by the power of God's love and walk forward in faith with the power of the Gospel!

Guilt

He has made us competent as ministers of a new covenant—not of the letter but of the Spirit; for the letter kills, but the Spirit gives life. **2 Corinthians 3:6**

There is no taskmaster worse than guilt. Guilt is tied to a religious spirit which can do a lot of harm to our lives and our witness.

My wife and I were discussing some opportunities that I had recently had to share the Gospel with people in my life. She then said, "Jesse, I think this needs to become less *duty* and more *love* in your life." Her words have really stuck with me. It is an honor to share the most beautiful message in the world, not drudgery! Why do we so often act like evangelism is our painful duty, a sad obligation?

The Scripture does not teach us to do things out of guilt. In fact, it says that Jesus has "cleansed our hearts from a guilty conscience" (Hebrews 10:22). So, what about all laws and rules in the Bible? In the New Testament, Paul says this in Romans 13:8:

> *Let no debt remain outstanding, except the continuing debt to love one another, for whoever loves others has fulfilled the law.*

What is Paul saying? Simply this. We do not have to worry about a bunch of rules. There is no perfect way to do things. We are simply following the Holy Spirit, trying to love people. So, what about obedience and obeying God's command to share the Gospel?

Our next chapter will be exclusively dedicated to a discussion on the topic of obedience. Jesus helped connect the dots for us between motives and obedience with this statement in John 14:15, "If you love me you will obey my commands." It is simple. Out of our love for Jesus, not to avoid guilt for doing the wrong thing, we share the good news of the Gospel with others.

Bitterness

> *See to it that no one falls short of the grace of God and that no bitter root grows up to cause trouble and defile many.* **Hebrews 12:15**

I do not have time to make an exhaustive list of all the toxic emotions that can get lodged in our hearts, but we will round out our list with bitterness. In all my years of ministry, bitterness may be the most destructive force I have seen. If left undetected, bitterness will mess up your spiritual walk and stunt your spiritual growth. Jesus said, "For if you forgive others their trespasses, your heavenly Father will also forgive you; but if you do not forgive others, neither will your Father forgive your trespasses" (Matthew 6:14-15).

Whatever you do, ruthlessly keep bitterness out of your heart and life. This is what I have found: Many believers have just enough faith to keep Jesus as their God. However, deep down, they are resentful toward God for the things that He has allowed in their lives.

If we stay resentful toward God, it is very difficult to promote Him to others. I will not downplay the painful things that this life takes each of us through. Ultimately, though, we are all faced with a choice: Will we run to God as the Healer or paint Him as the bandit who broke into our perfect life?

How to Grow in Love

Jesus is by far our best example of being motivated by love as we share the Gospel. While I struggle daily to keep my motives pure, God continues to teach me how to be "rooted and established in love" (Ephesians 3:17). No one will ever have perfect motives in their heart, but anyone can grow in love to be more like Jesus. Here are three ways to grow in love:

Decision 3: Love

#1: Focus On What is at Stake

Set your minds on things above, not on earthly things.
Colossians 3:2

Penn Jillette, the famous magician, comedian, and outspoken atheist recounted a story of a man giving him a Bible after a show. Jillette went on to share why he believes that people of faith should be sharing with others. Listen to his words:

> I don't respect [people who do not proselytize] at all. If you believe that there's a heaven and hell and people could be going to hell or not getting eternal life or whatever, and you think that it's not really worth telling them this because it would make it socially awkward, and atheists who think that people shouldn't proselytize — 'Just leave me alone, keep your religion to yourself.'
>
> How much do you have to hate somebody to not proselytize? How much do you have to hate somebody to believe that everlasting life is possible and not tell them that? If I believed beyond a shadow of a doubt that a truck was coming at you and you didn't believe it, and that truck was bearing down on you, there's a certain point where I tackle you. And this is more important than that.[25]

Forget the claim *anyone can evangelize*—apparently *anyone can teach evangelism*! The atheist is teaching a master class on evangelism and he does not even know it. He says, "How much do you have to hate somebody to believe that everlasting life is possible and not tell them?" We can use this to help motivate us to keep going when evangelism is hard.

We tell people about Christ because we love them. However, when we keep silent about Christ, this is equivalent to hatred toward others! We should be moved to action, not silence. When we consider what is at stake, it really is a no-brainer to decide what love calls us to do.

#2: Try Tears

Those who sow with tears will reap with songs of joy.
Psalm 126:5

There is a famous story of a couple of young Salvation Army missionaries who were trying to reach a community with the Gospel with little success. They reached out to William Booth, the founder of the Salvation Army, to close down the new mission. He responded with a two word telegram, "Try tears." They did, and saw a revival shortly after.[26]

In short, I want to encourage you to stay committed to the place of prayer. When you are daily praying for and letting

God break your heart for the lost, it is much easier to keep your love for the unsaved strong. When we lose the compassion that God gives to us in prayer, we can often lose our hunger for truly reaching the unsaved. Keep praying, *even ask God for tears*, and love will certainly stay in your heart for those outside God's Kingdom.

It is not just tears for the lost that fill our hearts with love, it is the tears of letting worldly things go and spending time with Jesus. The best way to fill up our 'love tank' is by spending time seeking God. After all, the Bible tells us that God *is* love.

Thus, spending time in communion with Him is spending time with love. Singing to Him, talking to Him, listening to Him, and reading His words help us to learn the language of love. Most Mondays during lunch and into the afternoon, I spend a large chunk of time simply being with Jesus. This practice fuels my whole week. Fill your life with Jesus, and He will fill you with everything you need to be an effective witness for Him.

#3: Follow Jesus' Example

> *Greater love has no man than this, that he lay down his life for his friends.* **John 15:13**

The Scripture says in John 3:16 that God so loved the world that He gave His only Son. Love was the motive for

Anyone Can Evangelize

God giving Jesus for us. Love was also Jesus' motive for dying for us. Jesus, Himself, said in John 15:13, "Greater love has no man than this, that he lay down his life for his friends." What a wonderful verse that is! He was predicting His own display of love.

So, how do we grow the love that is in our hearts for the lost? By following Jesus' example. We choose to lay down our lives for our friends. Last year, I was at the gas station and remembered that I had not shared the Gospel with anyone that day. I was tired, and the thought of sharing with someone was the last thing I wanted to do. I fought the thought of taking the time to share, but finally caved in.

I walked into the gas station and took a few minutes to share with a young lady who was working the register. She said she used to go to church but had gotten away from the habit. I invited her to mine which was close by and encouraged her as best I could. I was exhausted but got the words out and felt I was obedient to God.

I had forgotten about the situation altogether until Christmas Eve service at my church when I looked over at the front row and who was there?! It was the young lady from the gas station! I was so surprised and excited. I walked over and learned that she was a cousin of one of the couples who come to our church. I love seeing God tie threads together in a way that only He can.

Decision 3: Love

I am so glad that day that I chose to follow in Jesus' footsteps of sacrifice. There is no sacrifice we could make for Jesus that is greater than the sacrifice He made for us on the cross. I am reminded of one of my favorite verses in all of Scripture ...

> *Very truly I tell you, unless a kernel of wheat falls to the ground and dies, it remains only a single seed. But if it dies, it produces many seeds.* **John 12:24**

There is something within the story of Jesus feeding the 5,000 that we need to grasp. While we like to focus on the small offering they brought, we have to understand that the five loaves and two fish

The five loaves and two fish were *all they had*.

were all they had. If you really want to start seeing people around you won to Jesus, you will need to give everything. Paul describes it as becoming a living sacrifice. Have you counted the cost of winning people to Jesus?

I have found that there is a special grace available for the painful moments. Find Jesus' eyes, but also look for the wind of His Spirit. Like Jesus, let love fill every inch of your heart so that you can become fruitful in your witness.

For Three Years Those Tears Haunted Me

We have established that the best motivation for evangelism is love. Listen to the testimony of James Lynch. James was raised in a Christian home but ended up an alcoholic, barely able to keep a job. One day, Pastor Lee knocked on his door. They sat together in the living room, with James having already drunk too much that day.

Pastor Lee shared with James how much Jesus loved him and how He wanted to save him. When James refused to accept Christ, Pastor Lee knelt down beside his chair and, with tears streaming down his face, he begged James to surrender to Jesus.

After finally turning to Christ, James shared his story with Pastor Lee. He recalls the impact of this pastor's love: "For three years those tears haunted me. Not a day passed without my seeing you on your knees, begging me with tears in your eyes to repent and trust Christ." Not only did James repent, but he began in ministry as well!

James continues, "I believe that if you [Pastor Lee] had not come by my home that day, I would be lost without God and already dead and in hell."[27] Only God knows what can happen when we choose to love someone far from God.

Decision 3: Love

Allow me to conclude this chapter with this simple verse:

Above all, love each other deeply, because love covers over a multitude of sins. **1 Peter 4:8**

DECISION #3:

I will establish love as the reason for my evangelism.

Grab your journal or your small group and come up with a few ways you can turn this decision into action that anyone can do. Here is one to get you going!

Anyone Can:
Write down what evangelism motivated by love looks like.

Further reading:
Secrets of the Secret Place by Bob Sorge
The Search for Rest by Bob Santos

For your playlist:
Costly by Harvest
All Joy No Stress by Rhett Walker (feat. Tedashii)

DECISION #4
Obey

"If a commission by an earthly king is considered an honor, how can a commission by a Heavenly King be considered a sacrifice?" [28]
-DAVID LIVINGSTONE

Decision #4:
I will obey God's Great Commission no matter the cost.

The different views people can have of God are fascinating. As I was talking with one woman, she stated that faith in God was nothing more than an "easy way out" of life's problems. God was someone to blame when things weren't good and a crutch for the weak. While my natural response would have probably been to agree in some way with what she was saying and move on, a different response rose up in my spirit.

I said, "Ma'am, with all due respect, having to answer to the Almighty King of the Universe for all of our actions and thoughts is not the easy way out." The narrow path is the path accountable to God. Running our lives as our own god is much easier than submitting to God. The "me-monster" loves to run the show with as little resistance as possible.

Leading a life completely submitted to God is our next step in establishing a lifestyle of evangelism. When we start our relationship with Christ, He becomes our Lord. He is to be our Master. He is very gentle and gracious in His leadership, but do not be mistaken—He desires to be in charge the moment we ask for our salvation.

Willingness could be considered the waiting room to obedience. When the prophet Isaiah said, "Here I am, Lord, send me," God responded by saying, "Go and tell these people …" Isaiah's humble willingness led to him receiving a command from God. God went on to give Isaiah a message to share with the Jewish people. After this interaction, there was a final step Isaiah had to take for God. It was obedience!

Decision 4: Obey

From *I deserve* to *I will go*

Jesus gives us a glimpse into the kind of obedience He desires from us in Luke 17:7-10:

> "Suppose one of you has a servant plowing or looking after the sheep. Will he say to the servant when he comes in from the field, 'Come along now and sit down to eat'? Won't he rather say, 'Prepare my supper, get yourself ready and wait on me while I eat and drink; after that you may eat and drink'? Will he thank the servant because he did what he was told to do? So you also, when you have done everything you were told to do, should say, 'We are unworthy servants; we have only done our duty.'"

In this short story, Jesus is confronting one of the biggest cultural issues we face today: entitlement. Have you seen the videos online of people flipping waitresses' serving trays or cursing at customer service workers? We want it our way, and we are not happy when that does not happen.

The statement, "We are unworthy servants; we have only done our duty," flies in the face of entitlement. We live in a day where the "I deserve" mentality is running rampant. Here are some examples of this line of thinking:

- *I worked hard today; I deserve a steak.*
- *I did a good job with my yard; I deserve some video game time.*
- *I have been diligent with my taxes; I deserve to find a loophole to save some money.*
- *I have done a lot for God lately; I deserve to sleep in this Sunday.*
- *I worked hard the past 3 months; I deserve a vacation to Tahiti.*

The **I deserves** are a fast track to the **I regrets**! The sobering truth is that the only thing we truly deserve is death and an eternity away from God. Romans 6:23 tells us, "The wages of sin is death, but the gift of God is eternal life in Christ Jesus our Lord." All this life that we get to live is by the grace of God, not something we deserve!

Joseph was an incredible example of throwing off entitlement. The colorful coat his father put on him was a coat of entitlement. Lots of American parents put the same coat on their kids. It takes a very intentional decision to take off a coat of entitlement and submit to God.

When did Joseph take his off? I believe he left it in Potiphar's wife's hand. He could have used a lot of excuses to justify accepting her seductive advances. *She offered. This is God's way of getting me a prominent position in Egypt. God wants me to have children, right?*

Decision 4: Obey

As Joseph left his cloak in Potiphar's wife's hand, he was saying, "I am doing this God's way. I do not deserve anything. I am his servant. My life is in his hands." What about you? Have you dropped your coat of entitlement and submitted yourself to God?

It is time to escape the entitlement trap. The prescription for this malady? Humility and *thanksgiving*. As we set aside time to thank God for His kindness and blessings, we can develop a thankful mind. A thankful mindset keeps the glory going to God instead of ourselves. Giving thanks counteracts selfishness, which positions us to be useful in reaching people for Jesus. It is from this place that we begin the exciting journey of obeying God as He guides us on how to reach the lost.

Finding God's Treasure

Consider a pirate and his treasure map. A pirate loves when he discovers that there is treasure to be found. Carefully, he follows his map, with attention to every step. Then, when all the effort pays off, he finds the gold he was seeking! The pain is worth the prize.

When it comes to evangelism, *people* are our treasure. Let's go a step further. **People are God's treasure,** and we want to see them like He does! The Holy Spirit maps out our path to find the lost people whom God wants reconciled to Himself.

Anyone Can Evangelize

I remember a time during the COVID lockdowns when God literally gave me turn-by-turn directions to a woman who needed to be reminded of His love for her. I was meeting some friends at Kohl's to try on suits for my friend's upcoming wedding. Right when I arrived, I noticed a woman thumbing through a clothing rack and felt a nudge from the Holy Spirit to go to her.

I put off the feeling and went through with what I needed to do with the suit fitting. My friends left and even though the woman was still on my mind, I headed for the exit. Like a good Christian pastor, God was calling me to do something, and *I was heading in the opposite direction!* However, something happened that I did not expect: the exit that I walked up to was closed due to the COVID restrictions.

God used the blocked exit to give me one more chance to obey. Reluctantly, I told God I would go, but because I did not know where she was in the store, He would need to lead me to her. Suddenly, the Holy Spirit became a GPS for me. I started to hear directions: *Turn right. Left. Right. Left.* And then, as I took the final turn, there she was…at the complete opposite corner of the store from where I first saw her!

I walked to her and simply said, "I saw you and felt like God wanted you to know that He loves you." She imme-

Decision 4: Obey

diately broke down in tears. As the tears rolled down her face, she shared that she had lost her son at a young age. She was in the middle of trying to buy clothes for her nephew, but the pain of her son's loss was making it almost unbearable. I took a few moments to comfort her and went on my way.

The way in which this story unfolded can feel a bit mystical. *The nudge from God, the turn by turn directions,* etc. The truth is, we see evangelism happen like this in Scripture as well. For example, look at what happens with Philip in Acts 8:29, "The Spirit told Philip, "Go to that chariot and stay near it." Little did Philip know, when he got to the chariot there was a man there reading the book of Isaiah who wanted to know about Jesus.

It gets even more crazy. After the man is saved *and* baptized, we read in Acts 8:39, "When they came up out of the water, the Spirit of the Lord suddenly took Philip away, and the eunuch did not see him again, but went on his way rejoicing." Philip disappeared and the man went away a happy Christian! Wow.

Sometimes God's directions are dramatic; other times they are small, simple steps. Whatever the case, we can trust that God has valuable people for us to reach. Our treasure map is the turn-by-turn directions given by God's Holy Spirit and His Word. If we want to help people connect to Christ, we must be obedient to the directions Jesus gives to us!

From Apathy to Action

Apathy is defined as "a lack of interest, enthusiasm, or concern."[29] Is there a better word to describe the attitude of a majority of the church when it comes to the condition of those who are spiritually lost? I remember talking to an older Christian man last year who found himself in such a place.

He said that when he first got saved, he talked to people about his faith often and tried to get them to put their trust in Christ. He was quick to obey God, and committed to sharing Christ with others. However, he said that now, he rarely shares anymore. He still attends and serves within the church, but he does not share anymore. Somewhere along his Christian journey, he lost his excitement for sharing the Gospel with the lost.

Here is the reality: the commands from Scripture are the same for every Christian from anywhere in the world at any stage in their spiritual journey:

- "Go into all the world and preach the gospel." (Matthew 28:19)
- "Come, follow Me, and I will make you fishers of men." (Matthew 4:19)

Decision 4: Obey

- "We are therefore Christ's ambassadors, as though God were making his appeal through us." (2 Corinthians 5:20)
- "Always be prepared to give an answer for the hope that you have." (1 Peter 3:15)

When it comes to this elder Christian, had he let the distractions of life get in the way of his habit of evangelizing? What had created this slow drift in the area of personal witness? The enemy would love for you to enter this drift as well, so slowly that you do not even notice that you are no longer making efforts to evangelize.

We must become adamant to stay strong in our passion for sharing Christ! We must stand opposed to any deception that would lead us away from Christ's commands. The best way to fight apathy is with action. Tell someone what God has done for you. Give someone an invite card to your church. Push your head above water and watch God's grace rush into your lungs. **Guard against apathy.** We may not always see the outcome right away, but we can trust Jesus as we take a step of faith.

When It Is Hard To Obey

Problems creep in when the directions are difficult or do not make sense to us. Anyone is happy to obey God when His Spirit instructs us to take the promotion at work or marry the girlfriend/boyfriend of our dreams, but what about when there is sacrifice involved? What about when the Spirit instructs us to go somewhere we do not want to go? Listen to this encouragement from Charles Studd, professional cricketer-turned-missionary from the late 1800s:

> *Sometimes I feel...that my cross is heavy beyond endurance...My heart seems worn out and bruised beyond repair, and in my deep loneliness I often wish to be gone, but God knows best, and I want to do every ounce of work He wants me to do.*[30]

The question really comes down to this: "Do we believe we know best, or God knows best?" I recall a time when it was difficult to obey. One night, my wife and I were preparing to watch a show that we had been carving out an hour each week to keep up on. As I was walking upstairs, I felt a sense that we needed to skip the show and take some time to pray.

As quickly as my flesh was dismissing the thought, I felt a wind of grace that made the thought unexpectedly attractive. I have had this happen before and know it to be the Holy Spirit adding blessing to a difficult task. We found ourselves places on the couch; I had bent to my knees, Rachel was sitting, and we began to seek God.

Decision 4: Obey

Suddenly, I had a great sense that my neighbors needed to hear the Gospel. I had tried unsuccessfully for a few years to look for an opportunity to share Christ with the bachelor pad next door, but tonight, the stirring was strong. In fact, as I was kneeling and praying, I had a vision of myself and the guys next door praying together as they asked Christ into their lives.

I put my coat and shoes on as I sensed an urgency in the calling to share with the guys (all in their 20s) who lived in the house next to me. As I walked across my lawn, God gave me an uncommon confidence that I was acting in obedience to Him. I knocked on the door, and Brian, whose father owned the home but lived elsewhere, answered. I asked if I could come in, and he obliged.

We walked down a half flight of stairs in their bi-level, which was essentially identical to my own home. These guys had quite a setup! Instead of a typical family room setting, they had a series of desks and tables in a U-shape, each with different monitors on them—some gaming, others watching a movie or show. I believe at the moment I stepped in, there were three guys who all lived there and a friend or two present as well.

My confidence turned to boldness, and I asked all of them to turn off or pause their screens. They all submitted to my request and turned to hear what I had to say. I stated that I had wanted to talk to them for a while now and believed that tonight was the night. I then gave my best five-minute sermon about the living water that Jesus offers from John chapter four.

I shared that you can look through the whole world, but you will be left empty until you find and choose Jesus. I then inquired if any of them wanted to accept Him that very night. To be honest, I was expecting that my vision of us kneeling together would come to pass because it had been so vivid in my home just minutes before.

However, my message was met with indifference. They were respectful, but it was almost comical—my passion contrasted with their nonchalant response. Brian even commented, "I know that's probably not the response you were looking for but we appreciate you sharing." I responded, "I wasn't looking for any specific response, just your honesty."

He did add one encouraging note that suggested that this was not just a spoiled lunch. He stated that he had just started talking with a gal who was a Christian, and they were interested in dating each other. He added that she had just been sharing some of this with him when they had seen each other the previous weekend. I chatted a while longer with the guys, building a small connection after I had invited myself in and turned their

Decision 4: Obey

game night into an impromptu church service. Then, I walked home.

As soon as I got in the door, I got down on my knees to pray over the situation and for their eternities. Suddenly, I felt a nudge from the Holy Spirit to send a follow up text asking if they would do a Bible Study with me. I resisted because I was convinced that the apathy they had just shown to the things of God would certainly rule out their interest in a Bible Study. However, the prompting was strong, and I caved to the strength of the Holy Spirit.

To my surprise, after sending the text, one of my neighbors (Brian) responded immediately that he was interested! This began a six-month weekly Bible Study through the Gospel of Luke. Near the end of our study, he knelt with me in my living room and prayed to accept Christ as his Savior. To my knowledge, the others have yet to surrender to Christ. Lord willing, they will join Brian one day soon. Obedience can be hard, but it sure is rewarding!

This story has continued to bring lots of rewards and joy. A couple years ago, I had the honor of officiating the marriage of Brian and his wife, Leah. Further, just before I relocated to the Greater Cleveland area from Detroit, they moved into their first home in the same region. Brian and I are now neighbors (now a few miles instead of a few feet) in Cleveland rather than Detroit. Our families spent time together at the zoo this past summer. This story demonstrates once again that God knows best!

Trust and Obey

In chapter two, we looked at the prayer life of David Wilkerson. Now, I want you to see how he responded to God in obedience. After he had received the word from God to go to New York and help the gang members, he asked his church to receive an offering for him and his youth pastor to travel to NYC and attend the trial. They collected just enough money for him to make it to New York.

Miraculously, he and his youth pastor secured the last two seats in the courtroom. After the trial, Wilkerson holding his Bible approached the judge, stating that he was an ordained minister and asking if he could speak to the boys. The judge was unmoved that he was an ordained minister; and due to the publicity surrounding the trial, he had him removed from the courtroom.

Not only was Wilkerson prevented from speaking to the boys, but his picture appeared in newspapers across the country the following morning. The coverage was unfavorable, with the headline reading: Crazed Pastor Disrupts Trial. Even though many people close to him

Decision 4: Obey

condemned him for his "foolish" actions, Wilkerson felt God's leading to go back to NYC.

One night at his parents' house, Wilkerson told his mother that He felt called to return. She encouraged him to follow God's leading. Despite the pressure from the city and many others, he asked for another financial offering from his church to return to NYC. He made the decision to trust and obey God, even when it was difficult.

And there he landed, parking his car at a random street corner, not sure what to do next. As he stepped out of his car, two boys started walking toward him. They said, "Hey, aren't you the preacher from the newspaper who interrupted the trial?" "Yes," Wilkerson responded. "Come on over here, the cops don't like us either!" This was Wilkerson's first connection to the youth on the streets of NYC. In the years to come, he was able to build relationships with many of the gang members, hold evangelistic meetings, and establish the first Teen Challenge.

Even if your obedience ruffles feathers, runs against popular opinion, or does not make sense to you, do not be afraid to step out for God. Our obedience is the precursor to God's miraculous power to save the lost. Obedience may be difficult at times. It may feel like we have better things or more enjoyable things we could be doing. However, when we dig deep and obey our commission from God to keep sharing

Jesus, we will reap a harvest in due time! The reactions of others will vary, but we can rest assured God is pleased when we talk about His son to others.

Obedience > Outcomes

When we seek to obey, it is important to remember that we do not have control over the outcomes. The fruitfulness of our efforts belongs to God and is not something we always get to see. When we build something, we expect to be able to see the finished product. This makes sense when we are the builder.

God is the builder of His Kingdom. An electrician may not see the finished building, but he needs to do his job well. Can you and I come to a place where we are focused on doing our part well and letting God be the architect of His Kingdom? I can recall two examples of evangelistic efforts with very *different* results.

When my boss at a former job was retiring, I gave him a Billy Graham devotional book as a gift at his retirement party. I was not sure how he would respond, but I gave him the gift in faith that it would make an impact in his life. He came to me a few days later and was thrilled by the present. He told me that he had grown up watching Billy Graham's evangelistic crusades on television as a child, and now he planned to read the devotions each morning!

Decision 4: Obey

Another time, I had a neighbor who lived a few doors down who I desperately wanted to come to faith in Christ. We had talked a few times but had only skimmed the surface of spiritual conversation. I left him with a book in his mailbox with a note. It was a book that explored faith, and my note was a kind, simple encouragement to enjoy the book as he continued his faith journey. This time, I received a different reception. I found the book in my own mailbox the next day with a note that said, "No thank you!"

Both times, I gave a book about Christ in faith, obeying the Great Commission. However, I experienced very different results! This reaffirms the truth that obedience is up to us and the results are up to God. We must always remember that while we are called to obey, the advance of the Kingdom belongs to God alone!

> **Obedience is up to us and the results are up to God.**

Rejecting Rejection

I will never forget one of the first times I ever tried to share the Gospel. I was about 18 years old and was at Starbucks. I saw a man across the coffee shop and had the desire to share a Scripture with him. I got the Scripture verse ready and gathered up the courage to walk across the room to speak to him. I said, "Hi, my name is Jesse. I had a Bible verse that I thought would encourage you today and I am wondering if I can share it with you." He looked at me plainly and said, "No."

That was it. Just like that, I was walking away. I felt as if the man had splashed the cup of coffee in his hand into my face. I remember the questions that flooded my mind after that encounter. *Did God ask me to do that or was it just me conjuring it up? Should I have approached him differently? Why did God let me get rejected like that? Will God still use that encounter to show the man that a Christian noticed him and cared? Will that do more harm to the chances of that man accepting the Gospel in the future?*

Allow me to tell you what I did from there. After taking some time to process and pray, I made a decision: I am going to *keep going*.

I am not going to be swayed by people's responses. I am going to be guided by God's Word. Jesus said that if someone does not accept the Gospel, we are to shake the dust off our feet. So, that is what I am determined to do in those situations—not in an effort to be rude to people who do not want to hear about Christ, but to keep myself moving forward. It is a lot like fishing: you need to cast a lot of lines to catch one.

Decision 4: Obey

I do not know what your experience with evangelism has been. Maybe it has been really positive and you wanted to read this book as a tune-up. On the other hand, maybe it has been a series of rejections like one of my experiences was. Possibly, when you were first saved, you shared often but you have cooled off and need to reignite that first-love passion to share what God has done in your life. Wherever you are in your journey, will you join me in this resolute decision to keep going for Jesus?

I am going to *keep going*.

Can I tell you something really encouraging? After countless conversations since then, I have found that this man's response has been the exception and not the rule. Most people are very open to having someone share something spiritual with them. In fact, a recent survey found that two out of three Americans (66%) say they're at least open to having a conversation about faith with a friend.[31]

People are very open to having conversations about their faith, especially when we approach them with kindness and grace. At the end of the day, it truly is about obedience. We obey the Great Commission in faith. Sometimes we are rejected, but we embrace that risk, knowing that some will accept Christ and be changed forever!

Bring Your Five Loaves and Two Fish

One day, I was re-reading the story of the five loaves and two fish. I was once again captivated by Jesus' power to use such a small offering to feed over 5,000 people. As I meditated on the story I began having a conversation with God.

I said, *"We truly only need to bring our five loaves and two fish and you do the rest!"* The Holy Spirit gently responded to me, *"Yes, but many in the church today won't even bring me that."* This word convicted me and made me ask myself a question that I hope you will ask yourself as well. Am I too busy and too self-dependent to bring even my small offering to God? He wants to do so much but he needs our first step of obedience!

Listen to the incredible miracle God brought through a step of obedience from Lee Strobel, author of *The Case for Christ*. Since it is Strobel's story, I will let you hear it from him:

> At the end of a long day at the newspaper where I was an editor, I was packing up to leave when I felt the gentle nudging of the Holy Spirit. I sensed God leading me to go into the business office and invite my atheist friend to come with me to an Easter service at

Decision 4: Obey

my church. The impression was so strong that I figured something dramatic was about to happen.

I walked into the office. The place appeared empty except for my friend, who was sitting alone at his desk. "Perfect!" I reminded him that Easter was coming and asked if he would come to church with Leslie and me. He turned me down cold. I asked if he was interested in spiritual matters, and he emphatically said no. I asked if he had any questions about God, and again he said no. I explained why the resurrection was so important, but he wasn't interested.

With all of my evangelistic overtures being instantly shut down, I began to feel embarrassed. If God really had prodded me to talk with him, then why was he so uninterested? Finally, I stammered as I backed out of the office, "Well, uh, if you've ever got any questions, um, I guess you know where my desk is."

"What was that all about?" I couldn't understand why he was so resistant. I finally concluded that maybe I was going to be one link in a long chain of influences that would eventually lead him to Christ. Yet, as far as I know, he remains a skeptic to this day.

Skip ahead a few years. By this time I was a teaching pastor at a church in suburban Chicago. After I spoke one Sunday, a middle-aged man walked up, shook my hand, and said, "I just want to thank you for the spiritual influence you've had in my life."

"That's very nice," I said. "But who are you?"

"Let me tell you my story," he replied. "A few years ago I lost my job. I didn't have any money and I was afraid I was going to lose my house. I called a friend of mine who runs a newspaper and said, 'Do you have any work available for me?' He asked me, 'Can you tile floors?' Well, I had tiled my bathroom once, so I said, 'Sure.' He told me, 'We need some tiling done at the newspaper; if you can do that, we can pay you.'

"So one day, shortly before Easter, I was on my hands and knees behind a desk in the business office of the newspaper, fixing some tiles, when you walked into the room. I don't think you even saw me. You started talking about God and Jesus and Easter to some guy, and he wasn't interested at all. But I was crouching there listening, and my heart was beating fast, and I started thinking, 'I need God! I need to go to church!'

"As soon as you left, I called my wife and said, 'We're going to church this Easter.' She said, 'You're kidding!' I said, 'No, we are.' We ended up going to your church that Easter—and my wife, my teenage son, and

Decision 4: Obey

I all came to faith in Christ. And I just wanted to thank you!"[32]

You never know what God can do with a small step of obedience. Today is a good day to start! Take a step and see what God will do. Only God can save, but anyone can take one step … and that *anyone* includes *you*!

DECISION #4:

I will obey God's Great Commission no matter the cost.

Grab your journal or your small group and come up with a few ways you can turn this decision into action that *anyone can do*. Here is one to get you going!

Anyone Can:
Ask someone a spiritual question this week.
(See list of spiritual icebreakers on page 122.)

Further reading:
God's Smuggler by Brother Andrew
Under Cover by John Bevere

For your playlist:
Spirit Lead Me by Influence Music, Michael Ketterer

DECISION #5

Prepare

"In this day and age, evangelism is spelled A-P-O-L-O-G-E-T-I-C-S." [33]
-J. WARNER WALLACE

"It is not that D.L. Moody has more of the Holy Spirit than we do, it is that the Holy Spirit has more of him."
-CHURCH BOARD MEMBER

Decision #5:
I will prepare my mind and spirit for God-given opportunities to evangelize.

Anyone Can Evangelize

"Take a nap." That is some of the best advice I have ever gotten. It came from an older pastor who was sharing his wisdom with me. He said, "Sometimes the most spiritual thing you can do is to take a nap."

In this chapter, we will explore the vital question, "How can I prepare for the open doors that come my way to share my faith?" For the previous four chapters, we have essentially been doing *heart* preparation. To begin, I will make a quick comment about soul preparation. The bulk of this chapter, however, will focus on having a prepared mind and spirit. When all four (heart, mind, spirit and soul) are prepared and healthy, we set ourselves up to see some dynamic results in our personal witness!

The way I think about the soul is the culmination of one's heart, mind and spirit. It is the whole person. The best secret I have found to having a soul prepared to share Jesus is to ensure that your soul is rested. Having patterns of rest and Sabbath are essential to having a healthy soul. If you want to be an enduring witness for Christ, you will need to pace yourself.

I was in conversation one day with a pastor friend of mine who was around my age. We knew each other well and he had observed my passion for evangelism and the continual effort I exert to see people come to faith.

Decision 5: Prepare

He gave me this exhortation, "Jesse, remember even while people were perishing without Him, Jesus chose to take a nap on the boat. He needed rest too."

Instructions like these have helped me grow in this area, but believe me, I still overdo it often! I think as humans, something in us simply does not want to "stop". But it is important that we *cultivate* the soil of our souls. When you start to feel like a dry desert in the deepest parts of your being, take a drink of water (maybe literally) and rest up for the next day of work for God.

It is from the foundation of a rested soul that we can begin our work of having a prepared mind and spirit for evangelism. It is through both the mind and the spirit that people are won over to Jesus. Thus, we want to sharpen our mind and spirit as we aim to become useful to God. We will start with our mind and work toward our spirit.

When I use the term "prepared mind", I am referring to the work of intellectual training for questions about the Gospel. A conversation I had some time ago with one of my neighbors revealed my own lack of intellectual preparedness and has acted as a catalyst for defending the reliability of Jesus and His claims.

God vs. Science

Whenever I move, I thoroughly enjoy meeting all my new neighbors. A few weeks after moving into a new home, a neighbor from three doors down walked over. We were both removing our snow at the time. He was using his snowblower. I was showing off my muscles using my shovel (truth be told, our snow blower was broken). As we waded through the small talk, the conversation went a little deeper.

We agreed that we were both concerned for our kids in the current cultural landscape of our country. I mentioned that I choose to "pray a lot" for my kids as a response to my concern. There were a few other sentences volleyed back and forth, and then he made this statement: "I am not really a religious guy; I am more of a science person." I kind of froze. *We had just met, do I push back now?* I left it alone and we finished our cordial conversation.

Later, as I reflected on the conversation, I realized that even if I had wanted to respond to him, I did not have much to pull from. I was not studied or prepared enough for this opposing view. My eyes then began to see how often I received similar responses—not only about science, but any number of reasons *not* to believe in biblical Christianity.

In fact, I connected the dots to another conversation I had just had with a young man outside a Raising Cane's

Decision 5: Prepare

fast food restaurant. In our faith discussion, he made the comment, "Well, the Bible has been translated so many times, I can't trust it." Again, I did not have much to pull from in terms of a thoughtful, educated answer. I began to realize that my passion for evangelism needed to be teamed with knowledge. I believe God was using a series of conversations close together to open my eyes to the need for *study* in my life.

For many years, I did not like apologetics. For those who are not familiar with term *apologetics*, it is the intellectual defense of the Christian faith. Don't get me wrong, I enjoyed some of the talks I heard and admired those who were invested in the field of apologetics, but I refused to enter this arena myself. I did not want to study. After all, I told myself, *isn't salvation a spiritual and not intellectual thing?*

I have come to realize that that line of thinking was rooted in pride...and maybe a bit of laziness as well. Our culture is becoming increasingly more secular. On top of that, education has been elevated to a place of great honor and value in our society.

Therefore, we need to be able to engage with people's spirits *and* minds. Thus, I was convicted to enter the arena of apologetics, and I now believe that every Christian must spend time here. We need to be prepared to have the conversations that skeptics want and need to have.

Anyone Can Evangelize

Can't Teach an Old Dog New Tricks

I have often said that I am an old soul. In many ways, I wish it was still 1950. For example, I held out against getting a smartphone long after most of the world had made the switch. I clung to my "brick" until the world forced my hand. In my typical "old school" way, I have held fast for most of my life to my evangelism techniques as well... even if they are from the 1950s! I have come to a realization that runs in line with my realization about apologetics: Some of my evangelism techniques might be out of date.

Yes, I am having Gospel conversations, but I have had to ask myself a hard question. Am I actually reaching people? Let me give you an example. I have often used the "Two Questions" tactic, made famous by James E. Kennedy. It involves asking people a pointed spiritual question to steer the conversation to the Gospel: "If you died today, have you come to a place in your spiritual life that you are certain you would go to heaven when you die? The second question is "Why or why not?"[34]

These are great questions, no doubt. But here is the problem: The desire to go to a place called heaven—or even the belief that there is an afterlife—is far from a given in our current cultural climate. Many people are simply not motivated by this. In an increasingly secular culture,

Decision 5: Prepare

topics like sin, heaven, and hell, which may have been widely accepted in generations past, are no longer part of many people's belief system. So, what do we do?

First, let me make an important clarification: These 'old school' tactics can still be very effective. Questions that lead us to the simple Gospel are still good to have in our tool belt. As my wife said recently, "You need every approach when it comes to reaching people for Jesus."

My point is that if we want to be faithful evangelists, we must be willing to study the culture around us. The Apostle Paul said it this way in 1 Corinthians 9:22, "I have become all things to all people so that by all possible means I might save some." We have to remember that we are talking to real people with real questions who really need Jesus!

Translating the Gospel

The answer to reaching a changing culture is to learn how to bring the Gospel to them in a way they can understand and receive it. Just as I would not speak the Gospel in English if I were doing mission work in Zimbabwe, neither should we try to communicate the Gospel to our friends and neighbors in a "language" that they will not understand.

The Apostle Paul gave us a wonderful example of this when he was evangelizing in Athens. There was an altar in the middle of the city marked "to the unknown god." Check out the way Paul seized this opportunity. He says in Acts 17:24, "...the One whom you worship without knowing, Him I proclaim to you." He used their own belief system and presented his argument for Jesus in a way they could understand.

Paul leads the way for us. He translated the Gospel. Do some creative thinking about the opportunities that you can seize in your own context and culture. What open doors exist in your friend's secular belief system that are waiting for you to turn the key and present a compelling case for Christ?

A missionary leader told a great story of a woman who came to Christ through a tract she received. The woman grew up and lived in a country almost exclusively Buddhist. The tract that she was given gave simple instructions on how to pray to Jesus. The tract presented not so much a case for Jesus as Savior, but rather how to pray to the supernatural being and teacher known as Jesus Christ.

The woman read the pamphlet and said a simple prayer asking Jesus for a big-screen TV. She said almost immediately she received an answer from the new Being she prayed to: "Stop drinking alcohol." She stopped drinking that day and very quickly had saved enough money for her television. After some further interactions with Christians

Decision 5: Prepare

in her area, the woman accepted the One who helped her get her new TV as Lord and Savior of her life.

The Gospel was translated to her in a way she could understand, and she was able to come to a saving faith in Christ. In this case, it was through the person of Christ, and then she was able to learn about the rest of the story. Each person and situation can require different 'translations' of the Gospel. Let's look at some practical tools on how to enter conversations about Jesus and what to do once you are in one.

There are three keys I will offer you to help you have a prepared mind to translate the Gospel. If you grab hold of these keys, you will be ready to walk through the open doors in your life where Christ can shine in. The three strategies are:

1. Do not be afraid to argue (it's not as scary as you think!)
2. Ask good questions
3. Study opposing views

Put Up Your Dukes

Key #1: Do not be afraid to argue.

The best way to communicate the first key is with this simple statement: arguing is not evil. Arguing is defined as "giving evidence or reasons for or against something." Jesus and people's need for Him is worth arguing for![35]

Anyone Can Evangelize

When talking about evangelism in the Church, we have often been taught, "Do not argue with people." Anyone teaching this has clearly skipped over Acts 19:8 which states, "Paul entered the synagogue and spoke boldly there for three months, arguing persuasively about the kingdom of God."

Gregory Koukl, author of a great apologetics book called *Tactics*, makes this needed statement: "An argument is not a fight or a quarrel…arguments are important, therefore, because they help us discover the facts and find the truth."[36] The reality is that we argue all day long. Any time we are making a case that something is the right, most logical, or best approach, we are arguing for our case. Argument helps both married couples and organizations make good decisions. Arguing truly makes the world go 'round. We all have to argue every day.

Have we gotten fooled into thinking that when someone shares a view opposing Christianity, the most loving thing we can do is to 'just love them' and stay silent? Of course, there is a time for quietness, but let's keep in mind that often when an opposing viewpoint is presented to us, the most loving thing we could do is argue for the truth of Jesus. The next question is obvious: How do we go about this arguing?

Decision 5: Prepare

Can I Ask You a Question?

Key #2: Asking good questions

Ask good questions. This is one of the great secrets of evangelism and a great secret to being a good arguer. In fact, this is by far one of the most valuable sections contained in this book. The best example we have of someone who asked good questions is Jesus!

When people came to Him, He often asked questions instead of giving statements to start the dialogue. It is estimated that Jesus asked about 305 questions throughout the Gospels.[37] Here are some of my favorites:

- Who by worrying can add a single hour to their life? (Matthew 6:27)
- You of little faith, why are you so afraid? (Matthew 8:26)
- Which is easier to say, "Your sins are forgiven" or "get up and walk?" (Matthew 9:5)
- How many loaves do you have? (Mark 8:5)
- What does it profit a man to gain the whole world and lose his soul? (Mark 8:36)
- Who do you say that I am? (Mark 8:29)
- Do you love me? (John 21:17)

For someone who knew everything already, Jesus certainly had a lot of questions! How much more should we stay in a position of humility toward outsiders by asking ques-

> **For someone who knew everything already, Jesus certainly had a lot of questions!**

tions as our means for building a bridge. Remember, listening earns us the right to speak into other people's lives.

Here are a few questions that I have found helpful when transitioning into spiritual conversations. Usually, you will utilize questions like these after you have engaged with a person and developed rapport for a few minutes. These could also be useful when you are engaged in a designated time of "witnessing" with a group. Here are a few examples of spiritual icebreakers:

- Did you grow up going to church?
- Do you have any religious background?
- If you could ask God one question and get an answer, what would it be?
- Where is God in all the things happening in the world today?
- What is your favorite and least favorite thing about your religion?
- What are your thoughts about Jesus?
- Why do you think Jesus had to die?

As you develop the practice of asking good questions, it is important to become familiar with some of the routes

Decision 5: Prepare

people will commonly take as they share their spiritual experiences. Similar to the way a sports team studies game film for their next opponent, we want to be ready for what is coming. Let's dive into our last key for preparing our mind to translate the Gospel to those who need it!

Defeater Beliefs

Key #3: Study opposing views

Timothy Keller defines a *defeater belief* as "a set of 'common sense' consensus beliefs that automatically make Christianity seem implausible to people." If belief-A is true then belief-B cannot be true.[38] For example, if the Bible has been translated thousands of times, then Christianity cannot be true. And the list goes on.

Referring back to a Gallup poll mentioned in the introduction of this book, in 1965, 70% of Americans said that religion was important to them. However, in 2023, only 45% said religion was important.[39] This means that when we are trying to win our friends and neighbors to Christ today, we are often going to be met with a secular worldview. Thus, we must be prepared to en-

> **In 1965, 70% of Americans said that religion was important to them. However, in 2023, only 45% said religion was important.**

gage with them. Identifying and understanding cultural defeater beliefs is a big part of that preparation.

Remember, defeaters are beliefs that people in your culture have bought into which have ruled out the validity of Christianity for them. Here is my current list from my journal that I am studying through:

1. All religions basically say the same thing.
2. People only believe the faith system of the region they are born into.
3. Jesus did not raise from the dead
4. Organized religion is corrupted, only cares about money, etc.
5. The Bible is not reliable (ex. The Da Vinci Code)
6. Science and the Bible cannot coexist

Make your own list. Consider the defeater beliefs that people have presented in conversations you have had, and the ones you have been hearing or reading through books or media. Then, one by one, do some studying. Watch a video or read an article that addresses that question or issue. Pray and ask God for wisdom where the lies live in these false beliefs.

When engaging with people who present opposing views, the best response is often a good question. For example, if someone says, "I am not religious." You can respond

Decision 5: Prepare

with the simple question, "What do you mean by religious?" If someone says the Bible is not reliable, you can ask "Why?" and "Have you ever read the Bible?" Going back to the story at the beginning of this chapter, we can ask the person who says they are a "science" person, "Where do you see science and God in disagreement?"

People Not Problems

It is important to note that often people who present a strong argument against Christianity are masking a wound. There was a young believer who lived in the southern part of the United States who was engaged in conversation with a man he had recently met. As they began discussing faith, the Christian received this response from the other man: "I am more of a science person." The young Christ follower kept digging, asking about the religious background of the older man he was seeking to evangelize.

He discovered that the man *did* have a religious background, but a moment along the way had ruined his trust in religious leaders. He went to a private school and one of the teachers had acted inappropriately toward him. This created an irreconcilable divide in the man's mind. His conclusion was that if the 'man of faith' is corrupt, the faith itself must be corrupt.

Anyone Can Evangelize

The believer did not convert him to Christ in that moment, but he was able to pour some salve in the wound. He apologized for the religious leaders' actions toward the man. He took time to listen and encourage him. The younger man was able to share how Christ had done good things in his family and personal life. The believer did what he could, knowing that prayer was needed from the end of that conversation.

Here is our takeaway from this story: argue with all zeal, but do not forget that we are talking to people who need love, not problems that need solving! I find that the middle ground between grace and truth is love. So, discern what is needed and be bold to execute. Developing a prepared mind is the way to be ready to discern what is needed in any given conversation.

One vital note as you set your mind to this kind of preparation: The ultimate goal is to share the Gospel in our conversations. This does not always happen, but it is our goal. The devil has people blinded to the Gospel with all kinds of lies and false worldviews. We love people, so we walk down these side roads with them. Many have sincere questions. But keep Romans 1:16 as your bedrock, "For I am not ashamed of the gospel, because it is the power of God that brings salvation to everyone who believes: first to the Jew, then to the Gentile."

Decision 5: Prepare

The Holy Spirit will be our guide to find the open spaces in conversations to shed light on who Jesus is and why what He did on the cross matters. While the mind is a critical place for preparing to engage with people about faith, the spirit may be even more important. So, how do we prepare our spirit for encounters with nonbelievers?

Preparing Your Spirit

For most of my life, my father lived very close to me. He was either in the same city or a neighboring city, and I saw and talked to him often. Now, I live in Greater Cleveland, and he lives about seven hours away in Northern Michigan. This has made his visits and our time together much more meaningful because they are so rare.

Last year, we were having lunch when he was in town, and he said something to me that left a lasting impression on me. I was venting to him about trying to manage my life filled with ministry responsibilities, marriage, five young children, and a myriad of other demands. He looked at me from across the table at the hole-in-the-wall diner we were sitting at and took a few moments to silently collect his thoughts. Then he said these words: "Jesse, you need to ask the Holy Spirit to fill you every day. You will not be able to do all this on your own."

Anyone Can Evangelize

He was right, and I have been so thankful for these words of wisdom. As we look at how to prepare our spirit for opportunities to share the Gospel, the answer is very simple: We must commit to often and adamantly asking Jesus to fill us with His Holy Spirit. When we are filled with the Holy Spirit, we will be eager to talk about the One we are filled with to the people around us!

Acts 1:8 says these words: "But you will receive power when the Holy Spirit comes on you; and you will be my witnesses in Jerusalem, and in all Judea and Samaria, and to the ends of the earth." Did you catch that precious truth? The Holy Spirit coming on us is what gives us the power to share Jesus with the world around us. I cannot emphasize enough the importance of taking time to ask God to fill us with His Holy Spirit. And this request we make comes with a great encouragement from Jesus: "How much more will your Father who is in heaven give the Holy Spirit to those who ask!" (Luke 11:13)

You may consider taking a simple challenge to set aside 3 days to make your only prayer request for God to fill you with His Spirit. In essence, you are saying to God, "Being filled with You is more important than anything else I could ask for." I've taken periods of time to ask only this and seen incredible results. There is a joy, peace, love, and boldness that only God can give to us, and it is available only through the power of the Holy Spirit.

Decision 5: Prepare

Spirit-Led Questions

When we are full of the Holy Spirit, things get really fun in our efforts to evangelize those around us. Jesus was full of the Spirit and the results were astounding! Let us not forget one of the most unfathomable verses of Scripture where Jesus said these words in John 14:12-14:

Very truly I tell you, whoever believes in me will do the works I have been doing, and they will do even greater things than these, because I am going to the Father. And I will do whatever you ask in my name, so that the Father may be glorified in the Son. You may ask me for anything in my name, and I will do it.

Clearly, there is power from God available to each of us to do extraordinary things for His glory. Believe it! There are moments in conversation that can make a verse like this one feel like the farthest promise from our present reality. It is in these moments that we can collectively say, "I need God's Holy Spirit!"

This story was one of those moments. Have you ever gotten a faith question that stumped you? This one hit me and left me stunned for a few moments. The woman I was speaking to asked, "When it comes to the three faiths—Islam, Judaism, and Christianity—are they not all the same? Is it not the same god going back to Abraham?" She continued, "You know, Ishmael, the father of Islam, wasn't he one of God's children too and didn't God bless him?"

I had studied Islam in Bible College and even explored some answers to the three faiths questions, but the timing and wording of her questions left me speechless. I was actually preparing to acknowledge that these were good questions and move on (A.K.A. you win this round), when I sensed the Holy Spirit begin to work in my mind.

Almost surprising myself, I told her that I had a few questions to pose back to her. I proceeded to ask her a series of three questions:

1. Could God bless someone who is against Him?
2. If one god has a son and the other does not, can they be the same god?
3. If two things are 99% identical, such as twins, are the two things the same?

She received the questions with a genuine acknowledgment as if to say, maybe the God of the Bible could be the one true God. It was truly a moment where we could feel that God had intercepted the conversation with His wisdom. Anyone can do what I did in this conversation because anyone can follow the Holy Spirit's lead. He is living in every believer that has called on Jesus' name.

Decision 5: Prepare

The promise in Matthew 10:19-20 came to pass in this situation, and I hope you will take hold of this promise for the opportunities God gives to you to witness that Jesus is God:

> *But when they arrest you, do not worry about what to say or how to say it. At that time you will be given what to say, for it will not be you speaking, but the Spirit of your Father speaking through you.*

I had been arrested by this skeptical question, and the Holy Spirit spoke through me. I praise God for that. Do not worry, God's got you. He wants people to know His Son.

"The Spirit Has More of Him"

D.L. Moody is one of the greatest evangelists ever to live. It is estimated that he led one million people to Christ. He also founded Moody Bible Institute, which has been a leading Christian college for decades.

One night, a church board was preparing to meet with him to prepare for an upcoming outreach campaign. One of the church leaders turned to another and asked in a cynical manner, "Who is this Moody? Does he have more of the Holy Spirit than we do?" The board member he was talking to turned and said, "It is not that Moody has more of the Holy Spirit, it is that the Holy Spirit has more of him."

Anyone Can Evangelize

May that be said of you and me. May people look at us and say, "Now there is someone whose life is governed by the Spirit of God." Preparation is an essential part of the process of developing a lifestyle of evangelism. God entrusts more to those who have prepared themselves.

The shepherd boy David was a great choice to be king because he had been preparing himself in the fields. The dead lion and bear are proof. Take the necessary time to prepare your mind and spirit, and watch God bring you people with whom you can share the Gospel with!

DECISION #5:

I will prepare my mind and spirit for God-given opportunities to evangelize.

Grab your journal or your small group and come up with a few ways you can turn this decision into action that *anyone can do*. Here is one to get you going!

Anyone Can:
Pick a cultural defeater to research this week.

Further reading:
Fresh Wind, Fresh Fire by Jim Cymbala
Forgotten God by Francis Chan
Power for Life by Jeff Leake

For your playlist:
Holy Spirit Have Your Way by Leeland
On the Altar by Upperroom, Elyssa Smith

DECISION #6
Relate

"It will not do to say that you have no special call to go to China. With these facts before you and with the command of the Lord Jesus to go and preach the gospel to every creature, you need rather to ascertain whether you have a special call to stay at home."[40]
-HUDSON TAYLOR

Decision #6:
I will relate with those outside of the church so that I have opportunities to share Jesus with them.

Anyone Can Evangelize

Rosaria Champagne Butterfield checked all the boxes. She was a poster child for progressive America. She was an English professor at Syracuse University in New York. She was a feminist. She was a lesbian and a champion for the LGBT movement. She also helped sponsor many of the student-led LGBT groups on her campus.

As she was working on her second book, which was set to highlight the dangers of the "far right" in America, a letter from a local pastor arrived at her desk. He posed a few questions to her about a recent article she had written.

She decided to call him because she figured a chat with him could provide a good research opportunity to acquaint herself with the culture and people she was critiquing. As she talked to him on the phone and began asking some questions, he said, "Dr. Butterfield, I think that question should be considered in front of our fireplace following one of my wife's good dinners. How does that sound?"

She accepted the invitation and began a series of dinner meetings with the pastor and his wife. What began as a skeptic doing research soon became a sincere inquirer learning about Jesus and the Bible.

In her book, *The Secret Thoughts of an Unlikely Convert*, Butterfield shares about the first dinner meeting at the home of Pastor Ken Smith and his wife, Floy:

Decision 6: Relate

"They were willing to walk the long journey to me in Christian compassion. During our meal, they did not share the gospel with me. After our meal, they did not invite me to church. Because of these glaring omissions to the Christian script as I had come to know it, when the evening ended and Pastor Ken said he wanted to stay in touch, I knew that it was truly safe to accept his open hand."[41]

Over the next two years, Butterfield read through the Bible more than once. She met regularly with the Smiths, deepening their relationship and asking more questions. Then, on February 14, 1999, she attended church for the first time and that evening accepted Christ as her Savior. What was the key to Butterfield's incredible conversion? Hospitality.[42]

Who Are You Inviting Over for Dinner?

The hospitality of Pastor Ken and Floy Smith is something that I believe is often missing in our churches today. Yet, it is a vital and irreplaceable key if we want to be able to win others to Christ. Have we gotten too comfortable and busy in our Christian circles to have time to invite those on the outside in? Not just inviting them to church, but inviting them into our homes and lives.

Anyone Can Evangelize

Listen to Jesus' call to radical hospitality in Luke 14:12-14:

> *"When you give a luncheon or dinner, do not invite your friends, your brothers or sisters, your relatives, or your rich neighbors; if you do, they may invite you back and so you will be repaid. But when you give a banquet, invite the poor, the crippled, the lame, the blind, and you will be blessed. Although they cannot repay you, you will be repaid at the resurrection of the righteous."*

Have we neglected those who are *spiritually* poor, crippled, lame and blind? Again, it is not that we have closed the church doors to them, but have we closed the doors of our homes and lives to them? Jesus set a great example for us as He ate and drank with people who were far from God. The old adage, "People don't care how much you know until they know how much you care," is often very true when it comes to evangelism.

Start with your neighborhood. My wife and I intentionally spend time with our neighbors and invite them into our home and invite them over for meals. This has opened many bridges to the Gospel through the years. In many ways, love is spelled t-i-m-e. Thus, we make an effort to give time and attention to those who live next door. Live with the faith that God put you in the places you frequent because He wanted to shine light there.

Decision 6: Relate

My friend Caleb developed a practice called *This Thursday*. Each Thursday, he and his wife would have a different co-worker over for dinner. Maybe it is time you pop your Christian bubble. What can you do to intentionally build relationships with those in your life who are far from God?

Developing an Emotional Apologetic [43]

Over 60% of US adults report feeling lonely. Those numbers are highest among Gen Z at 79% and Millennials at 71%.[44] Anxiety and depression rates are at an all-time high, with 50% of young adults ages 18-24 having reported anxiety and depression symptoms in 2023.[45] Do you see the opportunity the church has?

The world is leaving people desperate for genuine, caring relationships. And we have these! Many teens and young people are not asking, "Can I have four proofs for Jesus' resurrection?" Rather, they are asking, "Can your Jesus and your church help combat these suicidal thoughts I am having?" It is time for us to break

> 60%+ of US adults report feeling lonely. Anxiety and depression rates are at an all-time high, with 50% of young adults ages 18-24 having reported anxiety and depression symptoms in 2023.

into their isolation with hope, life, and an invitation into *real* community.

One of my neighbors, Kris, gave me the opportunity to break into his isolation. I was doing some landscaping in my front yard on the 4th of July when I saw Kris walk by for the first time. I walked over to him from my perch in my flower bed and introduced myself. I wanted to intentionally take some time to **relate** to this new neighbor, even if it meant leaving my own little world for a few minutes. And I am sure glad that I did.

Kris shared with me that he had just moved into town and was living alone in a townhouse just a few streets away from me. After learning a bit about his life and family, I invited him to church. He came that very Sunday. He began coming regularly to church services and our young adult ministry activities. On our way back from a Young Adult event, he shared the biggest hardship of his life. A few years back, his mom had taken her own life. He shared about the pain this had caused him and how thankful he was to now be part of a community that cared about him.

Since this time, Kris has continued to deepen his roots in the church. He has begun serving and joined a small group as well. One of my favorite moments with Kris occurred last year after one of our Young Adult conferences in which the speaker taught on the Holy Spirit. He told me after the service that he was planning on staying home and playing video games until I called and invited him to come. "I am so glad I came," he said, "the Holy Spirit is way more fun than video games!"

As Kris and I have talked through some of the fundamental truths of the faith, they have all been easy for him to accept. His biggest questions were, "Does anyone care? Can Jesus heal my broken heart?" Through you and me, this generation can get answers to not only their *intellectual* questions but also the deepest questions of their heart.

Kris is just one example of the many people that are searching for meaning in the midst of the loneliness and brokenness of life. And, can I tell you my favorite part about my journey with Kris? I made a great friend. Every time we see each other, we both grin ear to ear. When we get lunch, we have incredible conversations. Of course, Kris needed me to be obedient to God and invite him to church but maybe, just maybe, God knew I needed a friend like Kris too.

Love Releases the Anointing

A few years ago, I was talking with a missionary friend of mine. I look up to him very much as he has served on the mission field for many decades. He even told me that he believes God has called him to plant 100 churches in

Africa, and he is well on his way! As we were talking, I asked him how he thought I could reach a family member who is close to my wife and me. We get to see this person often and desperately want to see them come to Christ. His answer surprised me.

I thought he might talk about prayer and fasting, or maybe a way to preach the Gospel to the person that would finally "land". Instead, however, he simply told me to show them love. He encouraged me to find little ways to serve and love them. He said, "Go up behind them and just rub their shoulders." And he ended his encouragement to me with this statement, "Love releases the anointing."

For those unfamiliar with the term "anointing," I would define it as God's grace to accomplish His purpose. With that definition in mind, let's lengthen our missionary friend's statement: "Love releases God's grace to accomplish His purpose." What a useful principle when it comes to evangelism!

Recall 1 Peter 4:8 which confirms this point, "Above all, love each other deeply, because love covers over a multitude of sins." Before we preach, let's make sure we take time to relate. Several years back, one of my neighbors affirmed this principle.

Decision 6: Relate

I had tried hard to share Christ with Austin many times. I had asked questions, and he had even attended some Bible studies that his roommates and I were doing together. Nothing seemed to get through to him. He seemed overall disinterested. Finally, I decided to drop the direct efforts of converting him and just connect with him.

I knew he was a big Detroit Lions fan, so I bought tickets for him and me to go downtown to Ford Field and watch an upcoming game. We had an incredible time. We got to laugh, cheer, eat and spend quality time together. On the car ride home, he shared more of his story with me and opened up about his upbringing and tense relationship with his father.

After the game, he told me how much he appreciated the time. In fact, he mentioned how not talking about faith but just being together meant a lot to him. Quality time and attention can release God's anointing to someone's life in a way that words and rehearsed gospel presentations cannot.

If there is someone in your life far from God and you cannot figure out how to share the Gospel with them, maybe simply start by taking them to a ball game. Let love soften their heart, with the hope that one day truth can enter as well.

Spiritual Discovery Groups

If there was a time in the church when you had to believe before you belong, those days are long gone. Spiritual seekers today are coming with the question, "Can I **belong** before I **believe**?" It is important for us to create a space for people to do just that. We want them to know that we have left a seat open at the table for them. One survey found that 74% of people report a lack of belonging in their local community.[46] What an opportunity the Church has to give people a place to belong!

One incredible example of giving people a place to belong who have yet to commit their lives to Christ is through spiritual discovery groups. Spiritual discovery groups are groups designed to allow people a safe space to ask questions and explore the Christian faith. One study tracked 1,100 people who were involved in spiritual discovery groups. Through this research, it was discovered that 80% of those who were involved in the spiritual discovery groups ended up converting to Christ.[47]

> **80% of those who were involved in the spiritual discovery groups ended up converting to Christ.**

That is an incredible statistic! Why was the success rate so high? I be-

Decision 6: Relate

lieve it was because of the power of relationships. Instead of someone hearing the Gospel through a sermon or a one-time encounter, they had a place to talk and build relationships with others as they explored the claims of Christ. When the Gospel is presented in the context of an ongoing relationship, the odds are greatest that someone will commit themselves to Christ!

If your church does not have a spiritual discovery group, consider getting one started. Our church uses Alpha, founded by Nicky Gumbel, which has seen incredible results worldwide. The videos and teaching materials will do a lot of the heavy lifting for you, so you can partner with the Holy Spirit to facilitate a safe place for people to explore the claims of Christ. Take some time to brainstorm how you can help people feel a sense of belonging so they can process their commitment to Christ in the context of a relationship.

Big Mama

Brett Ray was a burnout. He listened to Alice Cooper. He did drugs. He was an outcast and he knew it. In fact, he embraced it along with many others in the 1980s. School was a challenge for him and his life was quickly spiraling out of control. He recalls no one knowing what to do with him and most of the adults in his life leaving him alone except for one person: Big Mama. Big Mama was his grandmother. She loved God and she also loved Brett.

When she was over at the house and Brett was up in his room with the door shut listening to his records, she would come up and ask if she could sit with him. She would come into his room and listen to Alice Cooper and take time simply to join in his world. She did not judge him or scold him; she simply spent time with Brett.

Fast forward to one summer in high school. His parents knew they were in trouble with their son's current situation. They were able to convince him to attend a Christian weekend retreat. He went, and through the church retreat, God was able to reach him. When he shares his testimony, he always talks about Big Mama. She kept his heart open to Christ because of her example. Brett now gets to travel and share his testimony with teens and people around the United States.

Who is someone in your life that needs a Big Mama? Who can you take a step toward and show unconditional, uncommon love to? There are Rosaria Butterfields and Brett Rays in desperate need of the love of God. This past year I wrote these words on my whiteboard: "Make friends before you make converts."

Decision 6: Relate

Often, we must relate before we have the opportunity to speak. Jesus set up dinner at Zacchaeus' house, then he talked with him. Once we have taken the time to build relationships and trust, we must be ready to share the Gospel. This is where we will head with our seventh and final decision: Speak.

DECISION #6:

I will relate with those outside of the church so that I have opportunities to share Jesus with them.

Grab your journal or your small group and come up with a few ways you can turn this decision into action that *anyone can do*. Here is one to get you going!

Anyone Can:
Set up dinner plans with someone who is far from God.

Further reading:
The Gospel Comes with a House Key by Rosaria Butterfield
Fit for Battle by Sammy Tippit

For your playlist:
My Own Little World by Matthew West
Isaiah 6 (Here I am Send Me) by Lindy Cofer

DECISION #7

Speak

Part 1: How will they hear?

"It must not be tolerated that Christ should be unknown through our silence, and sinners unwarned through our negligence."[48]
-CHARLES SPURGEON

Decision #7:
I will speak on behalf of Jesus to a world who needs Him.

Anyone Can Evangelize

Last year, I hosted a roundtable interview with our senior pastor and his wife. It was a question-and-answer time for our young adults group to "ask anything". It is amazing how much wisdom nearly 40 years of ministry will produce! It was a gift for all of us in the room.

We were laughing, discussing some tough topics and enjoying the roundtable. At the very end of the conversation, someone asked this question: "How can I learn to share my faith with my friends or coworkers?"

I will never forget Pastor Kevin's answer. He said, "For me, I want evangelism to be my lifestyle… not a compartment of life but who I am. If you cut me, I bleed Jesus. It's who I am, not what I do."

The truth is, if you find yourself in a place where you are having trouble speaking to others about Jesus, you need to take a look at what is inside of you. *What have you been filling yourself with? When you get cut, what do you bleed?*

Listen to Jesus' searching words from Luke's gospel: "Out of the abundance of the heart, the mouth speaks." Let's look at the context of this statement from Jesus in Luke 6:42-45.

> *"No good tree bears bad fruit, nor does a bad tree bear good fruit. Each tree is recognized by its own fruit. People do not pick figs from thorn bushes, or*

Decision 7: Speak

grapes from briers. A good man brings good things out of the good stored up in his heart, and an evil man brings evil things out of the evil stored up in his heart. For the mouth speaks what the heart is full of.

It is simple: The things inside us will eventually come out. Nobody accidentally evangelizes. It is a return on an investment. I am always surprised how much I talk to people about sports. It has made me reflect more than once, *how deep is sports in my heart?*

Take a moment to reflect on what is in your heart. What have you been talking about? When we have been spending time with Jesus and our identity is firmly in Him, we will have no issue speaking to others about Him.

If you consider everything you have read up to this point in this book, this introduction to our last decision was basically a summary. Here is the truth: we do not have an evangelism problem, we have a shallow Christianity problem... a discipleship problem. When we live fully devoted to Christ, evangelism is a natural byproduct!

The reason you and I are not sharing Christ may not be fear or a lack of training; it may be found in our everyday living. That is why our first six intentional decisions need to be made on a daily basis, culminating in this decision: *I will speak on behalf of Jesus to the world who needs Him.*

Anyone Can Evangelize

Ashamed of Him

It was a Peter moment for me. A moment that I denied Christ. It took place in the lobby above the tennis courts. I was chatting with one of the dads of our junior players. We were having a nice conversation about one of his family members who was on the pro tour. I forget exactly how, but the conversation turned toward faith. He began to share some of his thoughts on faith. I believe I shared a bit as well, maybe mentioned that my day job was as a pastor.

Then, he gave a kind of summary statement that unfortunately is becoming more popular in the world today. He said something along the lines of, "In the end, all religions are basically the same. It's about being a good person, whatever you pick to believe." And then it was my turn to talk, and I responded with, "Yeah." The man had to go and we parted ways. One word, and immediately I could feel the Holy Spirit burning inside.

What's the big deal with my response? The big deal is that I agreed with a lie. Therefore, I was a liar as well. Jesus died on the cross and rose again, and that changed everything, and I believe it changed everything for me personally and anyone who believes in Him, and my response said, "His death did not really matter."

Decision 7: Speak

That was some of the deepest conviction I have ever felt, and it came from an evangelistic opportunity. I had been ashamed to side with Christ when the pressure was on, and I felt it. I had chosen myself over my Savior.

Years later, I was getting a haircut when my barber made a similar comment. "All religions basically say the same thing." This time, I spoke up. I defended Jesus as unique in His claims. I gently pushed on my friend's statement, pointing him toward having to make a decision about Jesus.

What do you do when the tide rises in your spiritual conversations? Do you jump out of the boat, or do you cut through the waves with Jesus? If you have been a coward in the past, maybe it is time to allow conviction to spur you to action. It may cost us something, but we need to be ready to speak on behalf of Christ. Ambassadors are not ashamed to boldly represent the one on whose behalf they have been sent.

Not Helping Our Case

Is the church today ashamed of Christ? The latest statistics are not casting any votes in our favor.

- 62% of Christians have not evangelized in the past six months [49]

- 25% fewer Christians believe the Great Commission is their responsibility over the past 30 years (a drop from 89% to 64%) [50]
- 47% of Millennial Christians say it is wrong to share their beliefs in order to convert others [51]

We need a miraculous shift in the church to take place. We must leave our place next to Peter at the bonfire of denial and join him on the steps below the upper room preaching the Gospel to a captive crowd. In short, we need Christians to start opening their mouths so God has something to use.

> **Jesus' death and resurrection were public events that are meant to be talked about.**

You have heard it said that God cannot use a parked car. He can't use closed mouths either. Be the boy on the mountainside. Bring something to God for Him to multiply, even if it starts by saying "Hi."

Has our teaching from the pulpits often sealed lips further? Quotes such as "Preach the Gospel at all times, use words when necessary" have become quite popular today. Sure, it is a cute quote. However, quotes like this can easily become a quick justification for not sharing, even when good opportunities arise! Let's be clear, Jesus' death and resurrection were public events that are meant to be talked about .

Decision 7: Speak

A young man who I met last summer was caught in this dangerous thought pattern. He was working the front desk at a tennis club where I had just finished playing a match (I lost the match..but we do not need to talk about that). After he found out that I was a pastor, he was excited to share with me that he was active in his church and recently served as a leader in their Vacation Bible School program. I was excited to meet another believer as we began to discuss our journeys to Christ and the churches we attended.

The topic of evangelism came up and that is when he dropped the bomb on me. He said rather matter-of-factly, *"I don't share the Word of God with people,* I just try to be kind to people and live a good Christ-like example." Good on him for trying to be Christ-like, but my new friend was missing an essential piece of the Great Commission. Go and *preach*…making disciples and teaching them (See Mark 16:15 and Matthew 28:20). You have to share God's Word in order to evangelize.

Maybe this "wordless witnessing" is a backlash to the church culture in the 80s and 90s where preaching and witnessing were thought to be over-emphasized. Whatever the reason, witnessing without words is a companion to cowardice and not a "fresh revelation". Rosaria Butterfield's story shows us that sometimes patience is needed, but sharing the Gospel is always a "when" not an "if".

Yes, living a lifestyle that represents Christ is very needed. But we must fight against the notion that witnessing for Jesus is either words *or* actions. Evangelism must always be words and actions. Let's unpack that further...

Teaching Without Words?

Preaching and *teaching* have always been God's preferred method for sharing His Word and building His Kingdom. Go and **preach**...making disciples and **teaching** them (See Mark 16:15 and Matthew 28:20). Every prophet, Jesus, and every disciple preached messages to bring God's Kingdom into their earthly situation. You cannot get around preaching.

> **Preach** *the word of God. Be prepared, whether the time is favorable or not. Patiently correct, rebuke, and encourage your people with good teaching. 2 Timothy 2:4 (New Living Translation)*

Consider my part-time job as a tennis instructor. I teach private and group lessons to various ages. Imagine with me for a moment if I tried to teach people how to play tennis without using words...

I give the best demonstrations and am the best *example* but never communicate the principles of a successful tennis player. It would be downright silly to try to pull that off. No club would keep that kind of tennis pro around. Sure,

Decision 7: Speak

demonstration has a place, but words are absolutely necessary when it comes to teaching a concept or truth.

Now let's look at Jesus' ministry. Imagine if Jesus never communicated the Word of God. He healed, He held the little kids, and showed His compassion to all the people He met, but never taught, preached, or spoke God's truths. That would be ridiculous. Jesus is our example. If He needed to use words, so do we. In fact, communicating the Gospel with words is the necessary *follow-up* to communicating the Gospel with our actions and lives.

What's Our Job?

After 15 years of actively sharing my own faith, I have come to realize the root cause of why most Christians think evangelism is too difficult for them to do. Simply put, they think they have to do it all. Thus, the following logic is applied to the area of evangelism: If the assignment appears impossible from the outset, the assignment will be delayed and eventually avoided completely.

Here is what I mean. People come to faith in a three-stage process. The three stages are *Drawing, Wrestling,* and *Saving*. The problem is, most believers approach evangelism as if they are responsible for all three. The truth is, God only includes us in one of the three stages. Evangelism is absolutely going to feel impossible when you are trying to do God's job!

Which stage does God choose to involve us in? The *Wrestling* stage. And what is our job within that stage? It is three simple words ____ ____ ____. Can you fill in the blanks (no peeking)?

I have put these discoveries in a simple diagram that I like to call 'The Messy Middle'.

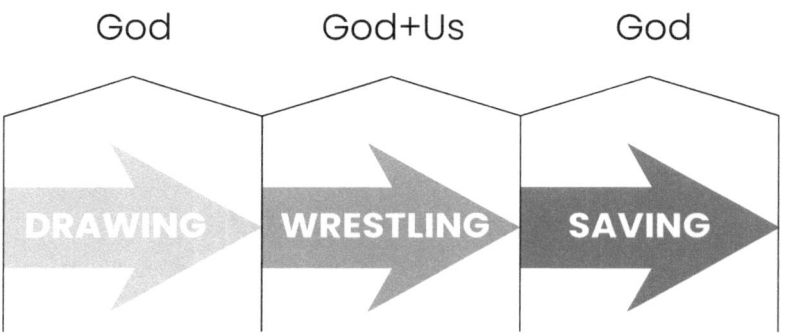

Our Job: Preach the Gospel

What is our job in the middle? What are we called to do in Scripture from cover to cover? What is the very first thing Jesus did on Day One of His ministry? What does the Holy Spirit use to reveal Jesus to sinners? What can anyone do to help someone wrestling with life and faith? **Preach the Gospel.**

If you read the Bible cover to cover, you will find the summary is as follows: Jesus Christ came to the earth to

Decision 7: Speak

forgive the sins of humanity, something no one but God could do. He died on a cross to take His creation's punishment and rose again to prove His power. Those who are witnesses that this story is true are instructed to tell those who are not yet convinced.

It is simple. God will draw and He will save in His way and in His timing. Your job is to jump in the messy middle with your friends and family who are not yet convinced that Jesus can rescue their broken life.

Viewing and Watching

We have become an increasingly *passive* culture.

Drew, one of the young adults from our church, shared with me over lunch an epic moment he took part in. He was recently at the movie theater when a man began choking. Thankfully, Drew was trained in CPR and had worked on a local EMS team. He sprang into action.

Heroically, while the man was having a seizure, Drew was able to clear both the popcorn and the man's tongue from his breathing passage. Drew held the man until the paramedics came. As Drew shared the story with me, he stated, "I was surprised by how many people just sat and watched."

I could not help but think that this reaction is a by-prod-

Anyone Can Evangelize

> **According to a Columbia University report, the average child (age 8-18) spends 7.5 hour in front of a screen for entertainment every day**

uct of the passivity of our culture. When there is an emergency, we are more likely to grab our phones and film it than we are to actually help. It is as if real-life situations blend into Netflix shows and we sit and watch, even in moments when we should take action or speak up.

Just take a moment to consider the major ways our time is spent: viewing and watching. According to a Columbia University report, the average child (age 8 to 18) spends 7.5 hours in front of a screen for entertainment every day.[52] This is a vital place where the Church must choose the narrow way and swim upstream. At some point, we must choose spirit over flesh and teach ourselves and our kids to look up because the fields are ripe for harvest!

One thing is for sure: the Christian life is not passive and evangelism is not a spectator sport. Bill Bright, founder of Campus Crusade for Christ (CRU), one of the largest college campus ministries in the world, said this:

> Whenever I am alone with a person for a few minutes, I assume that I am there by divine appointment to share the good news of God's love and forgiveness.[53]

Decision 7: Speak

We need that kind of active faith again in the church. Could it be that the opportunities are present, we just are not looking for them? We need to commit to being engaged and ready. As Peter said, let's be believers who are "always ready to give an answer for the hope we have." We need the attitude that says, "If I have ten minutes with you, I'm going to take the opportunity to tell you about Jesus."

What happened to our urgency?

Has the pendulum swung too far? Rewind a few decades and it seemed that every Sunday Jesus was "coming back tomorrow" and our neighbors were "going to hell because of our negligence." Maybe things went a little too far? Maybe the weight was unbearable, maybe it did not match Jesus' pacing? However, it is time to bring the pendulum back to a Biblical balance.

Have we lost our urgency to the point where we have lost sight of our mission and the need? Have we been lulled to sleep by other things and have we lost sight of joining Jesus to seek and save the lost?

We need to get back to a genuine, heaven-sent burden for the lost. We need to reignite the urgency, with a faith that does not skip over the reality of the righteous and the wicked. Every person stands face to face with two eternal options: God's judgment or God's mercy. You and I stand at the precipice of opportunity today.

A few years back, I was doing some street evangelism at a bus stop in Detroit alongside a gentleman named Steve from another church. It was a great time; we were able to share the Gospel with people while passing out hot chocolate as they waited for the next bus.

When I was visiting his church a few weeks later, I got to hear Steve's incredible story of becoming a Christian. He said that in his twenties, he was a painter. One day, while up on scaffolding, someone on the ground overheard a conversation in which Steve had been using several expletives with his coworker. The believer called up to Steve.

They said, "I am concerned about you. I have been hearing the words coming out of your mouth, and it makes me very concerned about your soul. You are going to stand before God one day and must account for the words you have spoken. It does not appear to me that you know Jesus Christ and how He can save you. I hope you turn to God."

Wow. That is a believer living with some urgency. When you lay out all the facts, this believer's conduct is actually very reasonable. And that one bold step from the believer has paid incredible dividends! They not only secured a convert but someone who has committed their life to fur-

Decision 7: Speak

thering the Gospel as well.

Take a moment to ask yourself, "Do souls still matter to me like they matter to God? Have other things in my life crowded out the urgency for the Gospel to reach lost people and change their lives forever?" If so, repent and restore your urgency today.

Repentance gives place to God's grace and encouragement. In Part Two of our final decision—to speak—you will find a game plan for communicating the Gospel. This game plan begins with a willingness to open our mouths. Meditate on Paul's questions from Romans 10:14 as we get out the whiteboard and lace up our sneakers.

> *"How, then, can they call on the one they have not believed in? And how can they believe in the one of whom they have not heard? And how can they hear without someone preaching to them?"*

DECISION #7:

I will speak on behalf of Jesus to a world who needs Him.

Grab your journal or your small group and come up with a few ways you can turn this decision into action that *anyone can do*. Here is one to get you going!

Anyone Can:
Explain the Gospel to a Christian friend
in under 60 seconds.

DECISION #7

Speak

Part 2: A Game Plan for Communicating the Gospel

"There comes a time when a Christian does not need another Bible study, another Sunday sermon or small group meeting—they need to go tell someone what God has done in their life." [50]
-GREG LAURIE

Decision #7:
I will speak on behalf of Jesus to
a world who needs Him.

We find ourselves in the locker room before the big game. The pads are on, the cleats are laced up, we have practiced for hours. We know the opponent is geared up to fight for their turf, but there is an electric buzz of belief in our midst. Something special is going to happen. We can win this game.

It is time to lean in to hear the game plan. Our evangelism game plan will come in three parts. We will start with a model anyone can use at any time called C.A.R.E. Then, you will receive a series of strategies that you can implement to carry out your God-given mission. Finally, I will share a few parting words as you take to the field.

C.A.R.E.

It is time for us to get practical. When those opportunities arise and we are in a position to have Jesus conversations, we need a base to launch from. In a recent survey by Lifeway, 66% of American Christians stated that they are not familiar with any "methods for telling others about Jesus."[55] Wow, what a statistic! There is no doubt a desire from many believers to share Christ, but there is a clear lack of knowledge.

C.A.R.E. is a tested and effective framework for sharing Christ. We will walk through a conversation I had with a neighbor as we learn this helpful acronym for engaging people with the Gospel.

Decision 7: Speak

Connect with the person
Ask a spiritual question
Respond with the Gospel
Exit with intentionality

<u>C</u>onnect With the Person

Practical: Connection usually starts by learning someone's name. I have found complimenting someone's shirt or shoes can be enough to make a connection and start a conversation. Get creative; remember Jesus asked a lady for water to start a conversation. Whatever it takes, try to get into conversations and meet people where they are in life.

Brian's story: The first thing I did when I saw my neighbor was reach out my hand. I had not met him before, and it was dark so I sought to make a connection by reaching out my hand. Once I had introduced myself and learned Brian's name, I asked some questions about him.

I learned that Brian was from out of town and grew up in Tennessee. I learned he was here with his fiancée, and they were expecting a baby any day. Notice, I did not start out trying to preach the Gospel. I try to make it my goal to make a friend before I make a convert. This doesn't mean I need years of relationship before I share; it just means I am going to find out about someone before I present Christ to them.

Part of the connection I made with Brian was finding out what he was doing. He said he was on his way to get some milk. I told him I would be happy to accompany him and make sure he knew which gas station was still open and would have milk. He agreed and we began our walk. This also gave me a guaranteed twenty minutes of time with my new friend.

Ask a Spiritual Question

Practical: You can refer to the ice breaker list from our *Prepare* chapter. Jesus did this masterfully. He would transition from the earthly to the spiritual with a question. There does not always have to be a perfect bridge though.

Sometimes when exchanging introductory identifiers with someone, I will volunteer the information: "My family and I go to a great church in our city. Do you go to church anywhere?" Break the ice. I have found that bringing spiritual things up in a conversation allows God to work in the conversation. It is hard for the Spirit to work if we stay on the weather and sports and never go outside the box. *Bringing God up, brings God in!*

Brian's Story: We were about halfway to the gas station when I found a creative way to turn the conversation toward Jesus. He mentioned that someone in his family was adopted. I then commented that someone from my

Decision 7: Speak

church was adopted from Russia. We bantered about adoption for another moment, and then I asked, "Did you grow up going to church?" This now fit in the conversation because I had just commented that my friend from church was adopted.

Once he began to share about his faith background, the door was beginning to open to share the Gospel. He said that he had gone on and off to church as a young person but had recently gone to a revival service in a city near his home. He went on to share that while at the revival service, he went forward and got prayer and felt something powerful he had never felt before.

Then, he asked me a question! He inquired if I was "born again." I was thrilled by the question and explained that I most certainly was! I then asked if he had been born again. He said that he did not think that he was but was interested. Now, the door was wide open!

Respond With the Gospel

Practical: As you converse with someone, look to the Holy Spirit to give you both an opening and courage to state the simple Gospel. The Romans Road remains one of the simplest, best ways to present the Gospel to someone.

One of the benefits is that you are quoting Scripture rather than just making up bullet points. If you have not already done so, I encourage you to take some time and memorize these four verses so you are ready whenever you have an opportunity.

Stop #1: Romans 3:23
"For all have sinned and fallen short of the glory of God."

Stop #2: Romans 6:23
"For the wages of sin is death, but the gracious gift of God is eternal life in Christ Jesus our Lord."

Stop #3: Romans 5:8
"But God demonstrates His own love toward us, in that while we were still sinners, Christ died for us."

Stop #4: Romans 10:9
"If you declare with your mouth, 'Jesus is Lord,' and believe in your heart that God raised him from the dead, you will be saved."

You do not have to use these four verses in full every time you are witnessing. Discern the moment. The Romans Road is effective because it presents the Gospel in a clear and complete way. There are four keys that you want to communicate when sharing the Gospel which are listed below. Practice sharing the Gospel in 60 seconds with a Christian friend so you are locked and loaded whenever opportunities come your way.

Decision 7: Speak

1. Sin
2. Repentance
3. Cross
4. Salvation

Brian's Story: I asked if I could share what it means to be born again, and he eagerly said he would like to know. I shared about Jesus' interaction with the religious leader, Nicodemus, in John 3 where the phrase originated.

"Unless a man is born again," Jesus said, "he will not see the Kingdom of God." I went on to explain that being born again primarily involves having one's sins forgiven, which was made possible by Jesus' death on the cross. And, I explained, we are only forgiven when we humble ourselves and apologize to God.

Exit With Intentionality

Practical: The way we leave Jesus' conversations is important. There are three places where I have found that every encounter will end:

1. Decision
2. Invitation
3. Reservation

Anyone Can Evangelize

When the fruit is ripe, ask them to make a decision. After praying with them, make sure they have a concrete next step. You should have a way to connect with them so you can follow up with the new Christian.

If they are interested but are in the 'messy middle', invite them to go further. Something to read, a group to attend, or more time with you are all good invitations. Have something to hand off like a church invite card or seeker's article in your car at all times.

Finally, many will resist the Gospel. With these, I sow the seed of the clear Gospel message if I am able and pray God moves their heart. I usually do not stay long in conversations when I discern significant spiritual resistance.

Brian's Story: He listened intently, but when we came to the end of the conversation, he was hesitant to put his trust completely in Christ. I asked if he wanted to pray to God that he would also be born again. He was unsure and said he wanted to learn more. I said that I understood because this was such a big decision.

I went on to explain that God made it clear in Scripture that there was a consequence to those whose sins are not forgiven, but that he had to come to faith in his own timing. As we closed the conversation, I offered my phone number if he wanted to talk further. He was very receptive and said, "I will come by your house tomorrow."

Decision 7: Speak

Here is what is really incredible about my journey with Brian. He did indeed end up coming to my house and spending time with me about once a week for two months. During that time, I focused on being a supportive friend. His fiancée delivered their baby, and he was going through lots of changes and challenges. I listened and supported as best I could.

Finally, one night we were talking at my kitchen table and the opportunity presented itself to revisit the topic of salvation. I reopened the conversation and walked through the Gospel with him, asking if he was ready to trust Christ with his life. He said that he was ready. We prayed together. My wife and I sat with him and celebrated together. It was a special moment.

I always keep in mind that I have very little control when it comes to evangelism. The only thing I can control is myself, how I treat people, and what I communicate. Their response and the fruit that I see from the encounter are God's business. Paul said it perfectly, "One plants, another waters, but the Lord brings the increase" (1 Corinthians 3:7). Commit yourself to taking time to C.A.R.E for people.

"I Want To Be A Witch"

I have become a firm believer in providing people an opportunity to say the "sinner's prayer". I will never forget a conversation that cemented this belief. I was on a walk

Anyone Can Evangelize

one afternoon on the sidewalk just outside our office. As I was walking near the main door, I struck up a conversation with a young lady who was standing outside the office building.

She must have been in her college years, and her wardrobe and jewelry presented a very 'new age' vibe. As we began talking, she informed me that she wanted to be a witch...but could not! I was intrigued, to say the least. She said even though she wanted to become a witch, something or someone was not allowing her.

She explained that when she tried to light the ritual candles in her apartment, they would blow out. Then, she shared her dramatic experience of the ceremony she had participated in to become a witch. She said that during the ceremony, a voice interrupted her very clearly and stated, "You belong to Me."

She shared with the witch she was training with what had just happened and what the voice had said. After some consideration, the witch stated that it would no longer be possible for her to become a witch. The witch said that the Being who thwarted her ceremony could not be overtaken. It was a lost cause.

I stood equally stunned and curious by her story. After a moment, I asked if she had ever prayed to accept Jesus

Decision 7: Speak

as her Savior as a child. She told me that around age ten, her mom had led her in a prayer of faith in Jesus Christ. Having grown up Lutheran, she remembered the prayer very well.

I started to connect the dots of what was really going on here. I explained to her that her Heavenly Father was protective and would not allow her to be influenced by other spirits in that way because she belonged to Him. She seemed to understand. I encouraged her to begin living for and believing in the One she had started a relationship with as a child.

If you have doubted God's love and power, just look at this example. Her story is a powerful demonstration of God's jealousy for us. Exodus 34:14 states, "Do not worship any other god, for the LORD, whose name is Jealous, is a jealous God." When someone asks Him to be their God and Father, He takes that seriously. He withholds nothing from His children and wants that kind of love in return. I praise Him for His wonderful character.

Can you see why this story has made me a big believer in the "sinner's prayer"? Some believers and ministers speak negatively about leading people in a prayer of faith in Christ. I disagree. Just like a marriage has a beginning point, salvation prayers are a starting point for new believers to start their relationship with God.

Anyone Can Evangelize

I am glad that this mother took the time when her daughter was a child to lead her in a prayer of commitment. Obviously, this girl (now a young adult) is having trouble following through on her commitment, but God heard her prayer and is being faithful (in the face of her faithlessness) to pursue His lost daughter.

I encourage you to ask people if they would like to pray to accept Christ as their Savior. Belief is backed up with our words. Do not be afraid to lead someone in a prayer of salvation.

For those who have never led someone to the place of salvation, this is not a complicated moment we are describing. What do you do? You ask the question, "Would you like to pray to accept Jesus as your Savior with me right now?" I have found that some people are literally waiting to be asked, and are thrilled to join in a salvation prayer. If the listener says "no", trust that they are not ready, there is no need to push. God will work after we have played our small part.

As a faithful witness, you want to provide new believers a place to become a disciple (invitation to church or time studying the Bible with you), but you are not responsible for their follow through on the commitment they made. You are simply asked to show them the way to Jesus. Anyone can do that.

Decision 7: Speak

Two Types of Evangelism

The reality is, there are two types of evangelism. One kind happens during a one-time encounter with someone, while the other is within an ongoing relationship. It is good to keep in mind which kind you are dealing with at any given moment. When you are at the doctor's office and sit next to someone for twenty minutes, the approach will be different than trying to lead your brother or neighbor to Christ.

1. One-time encounters

When it comes to one-time encounters, try to discern God's purpose for you in that particular assignment. You may simply be there to be a "rock in their shoe", challenging a lie that they have come to believe. Maybe you learn about a struggle they are facing, and you are able to pray for them. If they live in your area, you can invite them to your church. Look for a way to clearly explain that Jesus died and rose again, and why it matters for their life.

Whatever approach you use in these situations, I encourage you to try to make the most of the opportunities you receive. I keep Bill Bright's statement fresh in my mind: "I see every time I have ten minutes with a stranger as a divine opportunity."

Test the spiritual waters and see if God has something for that encounter. I have never regretted taking an opportunity to share Jesus with someone, but there have been many times I have regretted not taking an opportunity.

2. Ongoing Relationships

When it comes to ongoing relationships, the approach is often different. One thing is for sure: prayer is key to seeing success in winning the people that we are in ongoing relationships with to Christ. Keep a prayer list and commit to daily or weekly prayer for the relationships that matter most to you.

The approach I take with friends and family is to test the waters from time to time to see if there has been a change in their attitude toward Christ. Look for life moments that provide an opportunity to 'cast the line' again. For example, recently I was able to invite some family members to church for our Easter service, and they came and heard the message. When my children have been dedicated or baptized, I have considered who could be invited.

The list of other opportune moments is endless. It could be their life circumstances that enable you to show Christ by meeting a need, offering a prayer, and/or explaining why Christ gives you hope. There may be a time when you get significant alone time with them and you can go deeper than usual in conversation. Maybe you

Decision 7: Speak

can create a meaningful time with them by inviting them to do something you know they will enjoy doing.

I have also found that when one of the two is moving or transitioning, this can be a great time to share. For example, when I was moving from Michigan to Ohio, we had a mail carrier that we'd built a relationship with for seven years. After explaining that we were moving, I was able to express that there was "something I really wanted to share with you before we go."

In this particular instance, after explaining the Gospel, our mail carrier said she wanted to pray with me to accept Christ. I would like to believe that our family's testimony of joy and love had softened her heart over our seven-year relationship. God used our little family off Gainsley Drive to be a part of Tracy's story.

That day, in our driveway, she prayed for Christ to be her personal Savior! I gave her some additional information and told her about a good church near her home. Be wise. Be discerning and try to see where you can step in through an open door.

The 10 Commandments of Evangelism

Now that you have a basic model to work from and some

tips to use in conversation, I would like to offer you ten "rules to live by" as you seek to establish a lifestyle of evangelism. Some are reviews from other parts of the book, some are new. I will drop in a few comments with each one.

10 Commandments of Evangelism:

1. Ask God For Open Doors
2. Have Something In Your Hand
3. Relate Before You Propagate
4. Ask Questions
5. Go With a Friend
6. Use Your Testimony
7. Walk Them Down the Romans Road
8. Stay Focused on the Gospel
9. Invite Them to Church
10. Keep Fishing

1. Ask God For Open Doors

This is the starting point of evangelism. We are most likely to speak to others about God when we have first sought God for open doors and asked Him for the courage to walk through them. Begin every day with a prayer for God to give you opportunities to share the Gospel.

Decision 7: Speak

2. Have Something In Your Hand

I have found that having a pocket New Testament or church invite card in my hand helps me gain confidence in my witness. For one, it gives a place for my nervous energy to go! It also can give me a tangible starting point.

Sometimes I say, "Hey, I try to give one pocket New Testament (or church invite) away per day- will you be the one today?" Finally, it leaves them with something if they want to explore Christ further.

> **Begin every day with a prayer for God to give you opportunities to share the Gospel.**

3. Relate Before You Propagate

This point is review from chapter six, but it is an invaluable necessity in our witness. The other day I had a great conversation about Christ with a young adult in the grocery store. It started with me complimenting his golf shirt and talking about the PGA Championships that were happening that weekend. From that simple compliment, we ended up discussing where he stood with the Lord.

Look to go from the *earthly* to the *spiritual*.

In an age of shady salesmanship, it is important to build trust with the people we are engaging with. Sometimes I will say, "There is nothing in this for me, Jesus has just done so much for me, I simply wanted to share with you how good He is." Not everyone can do sales, but anyone can evangelize.

4. Ask Questions

Don't forget this secret. It is the number one way to move Gospel conversations forward and keep people thinking. Develop the skill of asking good questions—and listening to people's responses!

5. Go With A Friend

Things are easier when you are not alone. Jesus sent his disciples out in twos, so go with a friend. Recall from our first chapter, I only had the confidence to reach my neighborhood once I found a friend to go with me. Everything in life, including evangelism, is easier done with a friend.

There are other ways to utilize friends as well. You can create prayer partnerships for certain people that both of you are desiring to see come to Christ. Also, if there is someone that you want to share Christ with but you feel your relationship is not best suited for that conversation, you can ask another person to share with them.

Decision 7: Speak

For example, a gentleman from my church asked me to visit his dad in the hospital. He said that his dad was not open with him about spiritual things. When I went, though, his dad was happy to talk about the Gospel, church, and anything else I brought up. Often, "a prophet is without honor in their hometown." So bring in some back-up.

6. Use Your Testimony

Nobody can argue with your testimony. If you have not done so, take a few minutes and write out your story of coming to faith in Christ. Keep your story in your back pocket and use it to build the faith of others. Share your testimony with someone this week (Christian or not) to kickstart this habit in your life.

7. Walk Them Down The Romans Road

If you have not memorized these essential verses in Romans, flip back a couple pages and do that. This is the one of the best ways to share the Gospel in a clear, biblical way. Some people need to see it on paper, so open a Bible and show them! Use Romans 10:9 as a landing point for asking if they would like to commit their lives to Christ.

8. Stay Focused On The Gospel

There is a balance here between engaging where people are, and steering conversations toward the Gospel. It is important to keep in mind though, that until someone believes Jesus is God's Son who died for them, they will remain in the dark. The enemy wants to keep them distracted and keep their thoughts distorted about the truth of the Gospel.

You will often need to say, "That is a good question, but you need to decide what to do with Jesus first." I did this recently with an electrician that was doing work at our church. He was talking about what gender God is among many other unique and peripheral questions. I finally said, "Those are some good thoughts, but you need to decide who you believe Jesus is." I used C.S. Lewis's famous three options from there: Jesus must be either *"Lord, Liar or Lunatic."*

Keep your conversations focused on the Gospel trusting that is the power of God for salvation (Romans 1:16).

9. Invite Them To Church

The Billy Graham Evangelistic Association conducted a national survey and found that 82% of the unchurched say they would come to church with a friend or relative if invited.[56] When you meet people in your community, invite them to join you at church. You never know who around you has been wanting to find a place to worship or to learn about God.

Recently, I was able to invite my daughter's school crossing guard to church. She came two weeks later and said she loved it! She had been looking for a place to learn about Jesus

Decision 7: Speak

and was simply waiting for an invitation. Don't be afraid, and invite them in.

10. Keep Fishing

Do not get discouraged. At times, you will be rejected. Other times, the fish will bite but then swim away. Once in a while, God will allow you to make a big catch. Keep the Great Commission as your personal mission. Keep it in front of you. Stay committed to sharing Jesus every day.

> 82% of the unchurched say they would come to church with a friend or relative if invited.
>
> The Billy Graham Evangelistic Association

Now that you're equipped with strategies and wisdom for successful Jesus conversations, trust that the Spirit will lead you to the right tool for the right person. Take some time to discuss the Ten Commandments of evangelism with a friend or small group. Which comes easiest to you? Which is most difficult? Which one surprised you, and which one(s) had you already learned from experience?

Come to Me

Meet Afrooz, a devout Muslim living in Iran. As a young adult, she found herself under tremendous pressure from both work and school. As things got more complicated at her job, she reached a breaking point.

Anyone Can Evangelize

One night, she prayed to Allah and said, "I have prayed to you and you have given me no relief. If you do not show up and give me a sign tonight, I will become a heathen. I will stay up the whole night looking for a sign." With that, she waited in desperation.

Suddenly, as she was laying her head on her prayer mat out of exhaustion from the hours that had passed, a burst of light appeared in her room. However, it was not Muhammad's god who appeared but rather Jesus Christ. Afrooz shared that while she had never seen a picture of the Messiah, "I recognized that this could only be the Messiah."

Because Afrooz liked to write poetry, she always kept her pen and paper nearby. As the encounter unfolded, she quickly wrote down the words that came to her mind as she gazed at Jesus. She wrote in her journal these words [in Farsi]: "Come to me, all you who labor and are heavy laden, and I will give you rest."

Although Afrooz had this unique and powerful encounter, she remained a bit confused and still burdened by her circumstances. At work, a co-worker noticed her sad countenance and inquired. She shared some of her burden. Throughout their conversations, this co-worker revealed that they were a Christian.

Decision 7: Speak

Learning this, Afrooz pulled out her notebook and showed her new friend the words she had written during her vision several nights before. Her Christian co-worker then opened the Bible to Matthew 11:28: "Come to me, all you who labor and are heavy laden and I will give you rest."

This was the beginning of Afrooz's journey to Christ. Her believing co-worker helped fill in the gaps along the way. Can you see God's part and the church's part in Afrooz's story?

God did the drawing and saving, but her Christian friend stepped into the messy middle. God was already working a miracle, but He used the loaves and fish from the co-worker to give flesh and blood to the supernatural. Have the faith to speak into the lives of the lost because you *believe* that God is working behind the scenes. It is as if Jesus is beckoning the world to "come to Me," and He uses our gentle voice alongside those on their way to say, "It is OK to go to Him."

Begin with the End in Mind

Romans 14:12 says, "So then, each of us will give an account of ourselves to God." This is what keeps me focused when it comes to trying to reach the world with the Gospel. This reality of accountability to God on that Day motivates me today. Eternity informs my present decisions.

Anyone Can Evangelize

A good evangelist begins with the end in mind. We are often tempted to put off sharing the Gospel with someone the Holy Spirit is nudging us toward, but in view of eternity and the judgment seat of Christ, the logical response is to go! This temptation might come in the form of "wisdom" that says I do not want to bother this person. Do not be foolish. That is not wisdom—that is laziness.

Godly wisdom says, *this person may not know the good news of Jesus—I am going to make sure that they receive the chance to hear.* We must renew our minds.

Consider the parable of the talents. The ones who multiplied their talents pleased God. The one who buried their talent was cast out as a wicked and lazy servant. I sure do not want to be named with the wicked and lazy servants, do you?

The Gospel is the greatest treasure we are given as believers. We sell everything for that treasure (see Matt 13:44). Therefore, since we possess this treasure from God of the Gospel, He is looking to see what we will do with it. Will we bury it and put our light under the shade, or will we try to multiply His message and shine our light to the world?

Do not be intimidated. Make your best effort. Picture yourself before the judgment seat of Christ. How will you be found by Him? When you consider those around you whom you are burdened for, remember that they will face the Lord as well.

Decision 7: Speak

I was pulling out of the grocery store one day with my wife and five children loaded in our minivan. As we passed by a man in his truck with the driver's window rolled down, I felt a nudge from the Holy Spirit to speak to him. I resisted as I turned and began driving down the main road, justifying my decision to "be the good dad who gets his family home promptly." However, the Spirit persisted.

I turned the car around and drove back toward the truck. I pulled up to the driver's side window and told the man I felt the Lord wanted me to encourage him. He immediately broke down in tears, sharing his desperate family situation. I prayed for him and we drove on home. Eternity will move us to do crazy things! It's okay—Jesus dying on a cross for us is crazier still!

Beginning with the end in mind will move us to pray and preach like never before. Let's live with the goal of pleasing our Heavenly Father instead of people. When we stand before God, you want to be able to say, "Thank you for this treasure of your Son; I shared Him every chance I had."

Eyes on Jesus

As we bring our time together to a close, you may find yourself in one of two places:

Anyone Can Evangelize

#1: Overconfident - Ready to save the whole world tomorrow. You are already ambitiously writing the script to evangelistic encounters you are picturing yourself having.

#2: Still discounting yourself - You have read all the information, learned the tools, drawn from the stories, but you are still convincing yourself, there is no way. I can't actually speak up. This evangelism stuff is for someone else.

Can I share with you that both of these mindsets are wrong for one simple reason? They are wrong because the focus is on...**you**! I will never forget a rebuke that an 80-year-old minister once gave to me.

I had just finished sharing all the things that I thought God might do in the future of my ministry. After listening for a while, he said, "Do you know what word I have heard you say over and over again? 'I'. This is not about you. This is the Lord's work, not your work." I was very humbled and knew he had spoken exactly what I needed to hear.

Remove the magnifying glass from self and look outward.

Like every part of our spiritual life, the key is to focus on Jesus! Take the pressure off *yourself*. Remove the magnifying glass from self and look outward. Magnify God and the desperate need others have to know Him!

Decision 7: Speak

You will find peace and rest on the other side of this shift in focus.

Be encouraged by the story of Afrooz and many others. God will do the difficult part of drawing someone to Christ and the *impossible* part of saving their soul. He simply wants some partners along the way.

With your eyes locked on Jesus, bring Him your five loaves and two fish, and watch Him multiply your efforts. Simply make yourself available to our mighty God, and He will use you! With God out front, you can make a difference in the world. Evangelism is not for a select few. It is something anyone can do! Start small. Start today.

> *You know the saying, 'Four months between planting and harvest.' But I say, wake up and look around. The fields are already ripe for harvest.* **John 4:35 (NLT)**

Anyone Can Evangelize

DECISION #7:

I will speak on behalf of Jesus to a world who needs Him.

Grab your journal or your small group and come up with a few ways you can turn this decision into action that *anyone can do*. Here is one to get you going!

Anyone Can:
Share the Gospel in a simple way with someone who does not understand it.

Further reading:
Palau: A Life On Fire by Luis Palau
Tell Someone by Greg Laurie

For your playlist:
Go Tell it On the Mountain by For King and Country
Tell The World by Hillsong United

CONCLUSION
Do Not Give Up

Remember Tom from our introduction? Here is the rest of the story. God honored his humility in a huge way! Within days of me giving him that first pocket New Testament, Tom had a friend named Dacoda reach out to him. Although Dacoda was not sure what he believed spiritually, he was interested in checking out a church in the area. He asked Tom to meet him at a coffee shop and help him find one.

Tom told Dacoda, "If you end up at a church, someone is going to end up trying share the Gospel with you, so do you mind if I explain it now so that you are not surprised?" Dacoda agreed and listened to Tom explain what Jesus dying on the cross meant for us. They talked a bit further and then headed for their cars.

Anyone Can Evangelize

Tom said he felt a nudge from God to give Dacoda the pocket New Testament that was in his glove box. He ran over to his car to grab the Bible, then back to Dacoda. Tom opened it to the salvation prayer in the back and asked Dacoda if he was ready to accept Jesus into his life. Dacoda said he was, and they prayed together in the parking lot.

Dacoda shared with Tom and I that he kept that Bible in the pocket of his coat for months after he received it. He also shared that his faith went much deeper once he saw the kindness and care of the people at our church. Apparently, our example matters!

Update on Dacoda today...He is still serving Jesus and growing in his discipleship! After being an active part of our church and young adult ministry in Cleveland, he moved to Southern Ohio. When he got to his new city, he found a new church and plugged into their young adult group. He is a band teacher at a high school near Dayton, Ohio and tries to use his influence to represent Christ to the teens that he teaches each day.

Dacoda is now a light in his community because Tom bravely asked for help in the all-important area of evangelism! What an encouragement! As we bring this book to a close, I want you to be encouraged that God can do through you the same thing he did through Tom!

Conclusion

Ask God for open doors and the courage to share when they open. God will do the rest! Thank you for allowing me the privilege of sharing the precious truths and tools that God has taught me. I would like to finish by giving you a challenge.

The Jesus Conversation Challenge

As I mentioned in the introduction, years ago, I started making it my goal to share the Gospel with one person every day. Even if it was not a fully articulate, fancy Gospel presentation, I set out to pray with, invite to Church or share my testimony with one person outside the faith every day.

I called it the Jesus Conversation Challenge.

Since that first day that I started small, it has been amazing how God has gone ahead of me with this challenge. It is as if He wants the story of His Son to reach people even more than we do!! If you will wake up each day and ask God to open at least one door for you to shine your light, you will be amazed by the extraordinary ways He will answer!

I recall a story about two men who were at war when one was shot by an enemy bullet. As he lay in a ravine dying, his friend approached him, knowing that death was minutes away. His friend said, "Is there anything I can do for you? Any message I can bring back home for you?"

Anyone Can Evangelize

The dying man gave him an address and said, "Please tell the man that lives there that what he shared with me as a child has helped me in my dying moments?" Upon returning home from war, the friend made good on his word and knocked on the door of the address he was given.

An old man answered the door. The friend delivered the message. The old man looked up and said, "God, forgive me! I gave up teaching Sunday school years ago because I thought what I was doing had no effect."[57]

Friend, do not give up! Even if months go by and you feel your efforts to share your faith are making no difference... it is not true. Every seed of the Gospel you sow makes a difference. Some seeds bloom immediately, others take decades to grow. Be encouraged by Galatians 6:9: "Let us not become weary in doing good, for at the proper time we will reap a harvest if we do not give up."

For 90 days, would you challenge yourself to have at least one Jesus conversation per day? If you want to take the Jesus Conversation Challenge, I will offer a kickstart guide below. I am praying for you, and remember, God is with you. He can do a lot with a little! Simply bring what you have. It does not take a rocket scientist to share Jesus, anyone can evangelize!

Conclusion

Kickstart Guide:

- Take a week to pray and decide if you want to take the challenge
- Fast one meal that week to consecrate yourself to God
- Get a journal and write Scriptures/prayers throughout the week
- Commit to 90 days of Jesus Conversations
- If you miss one day, simply try to not miss two in a row
- Journal about your Jesus Conversation at the end of each of the 90 days
- Once you complete the challenge, consider making it a lifestyle.

Going Further

Going Further

Small Group Questions

Decision #1: Believe

1. What are the two core beliefs that you must have if you want to be an effective evangelist?

2. How have you wrestled with the temptation to believe that "all roads lead to God"?

3. Do you find it difficult to believe that God is preparing opportunities for you to share the Gospel? Why or why not?

4. As a group, take time to brainstorm more small steps anyone can take to implement the decision to believe (see page 48).

Decision #2: Pray

1. What makes prayer so important when it comes to evangelism?

2. What would it take for you to establish a habit of praying for the lost daily?

3. Which of the 10 secrets for praying for the lost stands out to you? Why?

4. As a group, take time to brainstorm more small steps anyone can take to implement the decision to pray (see page 70).

Decision #3: Love

1. Which of the heart detox motivations are you tempted to fall into most regularly?

2. How would you define love? What are the key characteristics?

3. Consider Jesus' example of loving people. In what way do you need to grow to be more like Him if you want to establish love as your motivation for evangelizing?

4. As a group, take time to brainstorm more small steps anyone can take to implement the decision to love (see page 86).

Going Further

Decision #4: Obey

1. How can you re-frame obeying God to be something that is enjoyable rather than something that is a 'chore'?

2. Has entitlement silently choked out your willingness to witness? How can we guard against entitlement in the midst of a selfish culture?

3. Share about a time when you obeyed God and you experienced a surprisingly good result.

4. As a group, take time to brainstorm more small steps anyone can take to implement the decision to obey (see page 110).

Decision #5: Prepare

1. What question are you most afraid someone will ask you when evangelizing?

2. What useful resources have you found for answers to difficult questions about the Christian faith?

3. How do you recognize when the Holy Spirit is leading your evangelism efforts?

4. As a group, take time to brainstorm more small steps anyone can take to implement the decision to prepare (see page 133).

Decision #6: Relate

1. What stands out to you about the pastor's interaction with Rosaria Butterfield?

2. What can make it difficult to relate to non-believers? What are some creative ways you have found to build relationships with non-believers?

3. How can you discern when it is a good time to turn a conversation toward spiritual things?

4. As a group, take time to brainstorm more small steps anyone can take to implement the decision to relate (see page 148).

Decision #7: Speak

1. Which part of C.A.R.E do you think you need to work on most?

2. Why do you think there has been such a drastic decline (from 89% to 64%) in the number of Christians who believe the Great Commission is their personal responsibility in the last 30 years?

3. Which of the ten commandments of evangelism resonated most with you? Why?

4. As a group, take time to brainstorm more small steps anyone can take to implement the decision to speak (see page 164).

Going Further

7 Decisions to Lead Your Kids to Christ

It is important to keep in mind that only God can save your kids. You simply want to be intentional about pointing them to Jesus. Here are seven intentional decisions you can make to lead your kids toward Christ:

1. Commit your kids to God

I was at a prayer conference a few years back when I asked God a very important question, *"How can I ensure that my kids do not walk away from You and end up unsaved?"* The Holy Spirit responded to me immediately with four simple words, *"Give them to me."* A.W. Tozer once said, "Everything is safe which we commit to Him, and nothing is really safe which is not so committed."

Parenting kids in a way that honors God is all about stewardship—managing something that does not belong to us. I have found that as I have transferred ownership of my kids to God, I have become more confident in my stewardship of their lives. Giving Him ownership alleviates the pressure. We need Him to fill in our gaps! Before further discipling your children, make sure you have given them completely to Him.

2. Make church a priority

I realized a while back that all the good things in my life have happened at church. I heard the Gospel there. I found my best friends there. I was mentored there. I met my wife there. I learned how to be more like Jesus there. I have eaten great food there. I have played epic hide and seek games there. I took a bath (I mean, got baptized) there. I found belonging and a purpose there.

I hope that you have also had a great experience with church. The church is the best group of people on earth and church buildings are the most fun and lively places to be. Make being part of a God honoring church a non-negotiable as long as your kids are under your roof.

3. When mistakes are made, point your kids to Jesus

While at a wedding, I met an incredibly wise, faith filled man. As our conversation progressed, he gave me a wonderful tip on parenting Godly kids. He said that when your kids make a mistake, the best thing you can do is point out that this is another example of why they need Jesus.

Before your kids make their own decision to follow Christ, use mistakes as opportunities to share the Gospel with them. Help them understand that our mistakes are the reason Jesus had to die on the cross! Next time your kid makes a mistake, help them to look up. Help your kids see their need for Jesus.

4. Serve with them

The last will be first and the first will be last. That is what Jesus said. If we do not teach our kids to serve others, we are in danger of making them into *me-monsters*. A great way to teach your kids to serve is to have them watch you serve others. An even better way is to have them serve with you!

Proverbs 11:25 teaches us, "A generous person will prosper; whoever refreshes others will be refreshed." Teach your kids how to be givers and servers. Also, help them discover their unique gifts and talents. When our kids begin to understand how they are wired and use their gifts to bless others, they are on their way to a vibrant Christian life.

5. Have dinner table conversions

The most effective way my wife and I have found to have meaningful dinner conversations is with the activity *High/*

Low. We go around the table allowing each person to describe their high point and low point for the day. There are so many good things that come from these conversations.

Everyone has a chance to be heard. We get an opportunity to celebrate each other's wins. We also gain the space to support each other in our disappointments. Anytime you can hear your children's heart, you are emulating how our Heavenly Father lovingly listens to us.

6. Pray and read your Bible in front of them

A common denominator in countless believers' lives is that they saw their parents practicing their faith at home. When you read your Bible and pray in front of and with your children, you are also increasing the chances that they will establish these habits.

Rachel and I have five kids and let me tell you, it can be exhausting and confusing. We strategically have Bibles in nearly every room of our home. When I "hit a wall" during my time at home, I find a chair and read a few verses. It is amazing how often those verses give me the strength I need to keep going. Let's model for our kids where to go when they need help!

7. Have fun with them!

Finally, make a commitment to have fun with your kids. Not only is LOVE spelled T-I-M-E, but it is also spelled F-U-N. I

Going Further

have found my toddlers nap better when I first take 15 minutes to play and laugh with them on the floor.

Fun has the ability to fuel faith. Fun builds relationships. Fun builds trust. Allowing your house to be a place of enjoyment will help your kids be more willing to do the hard things like chores, homework and going to bed. Laugh, snuggle, wrestle and play your way to a God-centered family.

7 Decisions to Create an Outreach Culture at Your Church

This section is primarily written for pastors and leaders, but I invite others to lean in and glean from these practical tips for creating an evangelistic or "outward-facing" church culture.

1. Preach evangelism and give regular salvation calls

Greg Laurie, Pastor of Harvest Christian Fellowship in Riverside, California includes a call for his church to evangelize in almost every sermon. No matter the text or topic, he looks for a way to encourage his church to be inviting people into faith and church throughout the week. Our people need to understand that Jesus' mission was to "seek and save the lost" and our mission is the same! They should hear this regularly.

Recently, I visited a church for the first time during a week of vacation. The pastor gave a brilliant sermon—incredible stories, illustrations and practical challenges. As he spoke about Jesus' disciple who he called "little James," he encouraged the church that God can use anyone. The table was set as he neared the end of his message for him to give a wonderful call for salvation. However, it never came. I was stunned.

This is a growing church, probably pushing a thousand people in attendance between all their services, but there was no salvation call. Preachers out there, please heed this instruction. Assume every crowd has unsaved people in it and take every opportunity you have to explain how people can be saved. It is your primary job. The rest is just the build up!

2. Host an annual "Party in the Park"

Pastor Kevin Crow (my pastor) tells the story of how our biggest outreach of the year started at Harvest Ridge Church in North Ridgeville, Ohio. He took his kids to the Rib Festival in Cleveland many years ago. He was hoping to have a fun night out with his family but came up very empty. He was disappointed after a terrible experience, spending way too much money for just a few activities, and being surrounded by drunk people. While talking to one of his staff pastors, the two of them came up with an outreach idea.

Going Further

They posed a few questions to each other. What if we gave the dads in our community an amazing night out with their family? What if we had games, bounce houses, face painting, hot dogs, and balloon animals? What if we hosted it at the park in the middle of town? What if it finished with a huge fireworks show? And...what if it was all free?

From that conversation 15 years ago, the first Party in the Park was born. This past Labor Day Sunday, an estimated 4,000 people converged on South Central Park for Harvest Palooza. If you want to become an outward-facing church, consider throwing your city a free party with the goal of simply telling them, "Jesus loves you and so do we!"

3. Plan a three-week intentional outreach

One of the best ways to see visitors become disciples is to get to them to come multiple weeks in a row. This might be through a series with a specific learning progression that new believers will be interested in. Another way to do this is through using a season of the year such as Easter to implement a creative three week run such as the one below.

Ex: Bring-a-Friend Day Sunday, Easter Egg Hunt (Post-service) Sunday, Easter Sunday

4. Make outreach not one component, but the attitude of everything you do.

There is a trap we can fall into when we make outreach one of many programs that our church offers. Rather, it is better to see outreach as a circle around everything we do. Whether it is an event, service, or small group we should endeavor to teach our people to:

1. Invite people.

2. Include the Gospel.

Some leaders call this having an "invite culture." Instead of only the community service project or street witnessing hour being considered outreach, consider everything outreach. Someone is always watching and there is always someone to invite.

5. Host evangelism conferences and training sessions

One of the most common reasons that church goers do not share that faith is because they do not feel that they know how. According to Lifeway Research, 66% of Christians say they aren't familiar with any methods of telling others about Jesus.[58] The truth is, every church has a simple solution to this problem.

Find the most well-equipped evangelist or pastor in your community and have them schedule a training for your church. It would be an honor if you used this book, *Anyone Can Evangelize*, as a tool for your church. You could use it in a small group or weekend training. The seven decisions, ten prayer secrets, ten commandments of evangelism, and the C.A.R.E. acronym and were all written in a way that could be easily broken down, taught and practiced.

6. Have dedicated outreach and prayer small groups

Look for the evangelists in your church. Yes, everyone is called to evangelism but in my experience about 10% of every church is people who are naturally gifted to share the Gospel and bring people to Jesus.

Establish a place where these people meet each other and start a group. In my church context, our group focuses on praying for the lost in the winter and going out and sharing in the summer. Ask God to send you a group leader who has God's heart for the lost in your community.

7. Start seeker-friendly small groups

If your church does not have a seeker group such as Alpha, put it on the top of your prayer list. These groups are essential in today's world. There are countless people who are interested in accepting Christ but have real questions that they need to ask. You can create a space for them to process through the Gospel.

Anyone Can Evangelize

Our church recently started an Alpha group after not having one for a few years. We have seen incredible results. Our life groups are making dinners for the Alpha participants. Each session includes a short video and time for discussion. Recall, one study of over 1,000 people who were attending seeker small groups found that 80% made a commitment to Christ!

Acknowledgements

This book is the combination of lots of hard work and about a hundred miracles. There are lots of people that have invested in my journey and this book. I would like to thank a few by name:

First of all, I want to thank Jesus for dying for me and giving me the gift and passion to teach evangelism. This book is about You, for You and I pray it represents Your heart well.

Rachel, thank you for supporting my writing and research for this book. It took A LOT of time, sometimes family time, and you stayed the course with me. You are a blessing.

Harper, Caleb, Millie, Josie, and Gabriel, my kiddos! Thank you for going on this journey with me! Also, Harper and Caleb, thank you for your encouragement along the way.

Anyone Can Evangelize

Pastor Kevin and the staff at Harvest Ridge. You guys are incredible. This team is so special to me and each of you have invested in me in a unique way to help me finish this assignment. Thank you for accepting me just as I am. Love you guys. Let's keep changing the world together.

Tim Twigg and your team at Arrow Press. Tim, thank you for coming alongside me to finish this book and get it out to the world. You guys are doing great work, praying God continues to trust you with more opportunities to advance His Kingdom!

Thank you to my pastors through the years. Kevin Crow, Tony and Chris Rea, Nate Peshl, George Johnson, and Dan Mastro, thank you for your love and care for my family and I.

Sean Terry, thank you for the help with the video. The only thing I love more than your talent is your heart for God and people!

Brian Loch, thank you for editing the trailer. You are the best neighbor I have ever had!!

Tim Warrick, thank you for offering to edit my first draft. Your encouragement meant a lot to me through this process.

Sara Hollifield, thank you for the website help. It is amazing that you had been doing web work with Christian authors for years before we connected!

Jonathan Rosa, there was a moment in the writing process where you came up huge for me. Thank you for your support.

Finally, there are a few friends that have given me strength through the whole project. Thank you guys: Steve Archer, Ron Bolden, and Jay Currie.

Notes

INTRODUCTION

1. https://www.christianpost.com/news/two-thirds-of-christians-dont-know-methods-for-sharing-jesus.html

CHAPTER 1

2. https://zondervan.typepad.com/zondervan/2012/04/unlikely-evangelist-moodys-life-prayer-spirit-excerpt-cymbala.html
3. https://en.wikipedia.org/wiki/Ray_Comfort
4. https://youtu.be/IAV76ah8N6Q?si=D-1sSXA2sD8eotM8
5. Acts 4:7b
6. https://www.preaching.com/articles/40-courageous-quotes-evangelist-billy-graham/
7. https://www.facebook.com/daveramsey/posts/90-of-solving-a-problem-is-realizing-there-is one/10157830079915886/
8. When Faith is Forbidden, Nettleton, Todd pp. 221-224, Moody Publishers. 2021

9. https://www.barna.com/research/rising-spiritual-openness/
10. https://www.jesusburgers.org/about
11. Adachi, K., (2021). The Lazy Genius Way: Embrace What Matters, Ditch What Doesn't, and Get Stuff Done. Waterbrook Press. p.41

CHAPTER 2

12. https://kiebowman.com/2021/08/
13. https://www.globaltc.org/our-history/
14. http://teenchallengehawaii.com/wp-content/uploads/2017/06/Success-Rate-of-Teen-Challenge.pdf
15. The Cross and the Switchblade, Wilkerson, David pp. 15-21, Berkley. 1962
16. https://marriageaftergod.com/prayer-is-not-a-preparation-for-the-battle-it-is-the-battle/
17. https://youtu.be/EDpxUecBOro
18. https://www.gracefellowshipofaugusta.com/pastor-brians-blog/post/encouraged-by-george-mueller
19. https://research.lifeway.com/2021/06/09/the-places-where-no-one-knows-a-christian/
20. Thomas, E. Lee. Praying Effectively for the Lost. (2003). Pg. 39

CHAPTER 3

21. https://afci.com.au/connecting-with-non-christians-makes-you-care-about-sharing-christ-with-them/
22. Carre, E.G. Praying Hyde p. 39 South Plainsfield: Bridge, n.d.
23. https://livingwaters.com/overcoming-fear-when-sharing-your-faith/
24. https://www.johnmaxwell.com/blog/making-the-transition-to-intentional-growth/

Notes

25. https://www.baptistpress.com/resource-library/news/atheism-penn-jillette-urges-evangelism/
26. https://thecomingrevival.com/william-booth-salvation-army/
27. Thomas, E. Lee. Praying Effectively for the Lost. (2003). Pg. 49

CHAPTER 4

28. https://gfamissions.org/high-calling-of-being-a-missionary/
29. Oxford Dictionary
30. https://www.azquotes.com/quote/757382?ref=god-knows-best
31. https://research.lifeway.com/2022/02/22/most-open-to-spiritual-conversations-few-christians-speaking/
32. Christian Research Institute. Experiencing Your Own Unexpected Adventures. Lee Strobel. Article ID: JAE325. www.equip.org/articles/experiencing-your-own-unexpected-adventures/

CHAPTER 5

33. https://coldcasechristianity.com/writings/in-this-day-and-age-evangelism-is-spelled-a-p-o-l-o-g-e-t-i-c-s/
34. https://evangelismexplosion.org/diagnostic-questions-2/
35. Oxford dictionary
36. Stand to Reason, Arguing is a Virtue, published on 5/1/1992 by Gregory Koukl
37. https://redletterchallenge.com/the-305-questions-jesus-asked-with-one-shocking-discovery/?srsltid=AfmBOor9M-ZaMxDdjoMS5fFvdHxd66F6mCSANUtnP2VGp4hOlAA6b8709
38. Keller, Timothy, Deconstructing Defeater Beliefs: Leading the Secular to Christ. Article published by Redeemer Presbyterian Church. 2004

39. https://news.gallup.com/poll/358364/religious-americans.aspx

CHAPTER 6

40. Thttps://visionforchina.org/the-china-missions-quote-project
41. Champagne Butterfield, R. (2012). Secret thoughts of an unlikely convert: An English professor's journey into Christian faith. p.11, Crown and Covenant Publications.
42. Champagne Butterfield, R. (2012). Secret thoughts of an unlikely convert: An English professor's journey into Christian faith. Crown and Covenant Publications. First three chapters summarized.
43. Term coined by Tyler Staton, https://churchsource.com/blogs/ministry-resources/how-to-reach-a-generation-on-the-road-to-emmaus-tyler-stanton
44. https://www.discoveryaba.com/statistics/loneliness#:~:text=Over%2060%25%20of%20adults%20in,smoking%20 15%20cigarettes%20a%20day.
45. https://www.kff.org/mental-health/press-release/latest-federal-data-show-that-young-people-are-more-likely-than-older-adults-to-be-experiencing-symptoms-of-anxiety-or-depression/#:~:text=The%20analysis%20of%20the%20 Census,a%20third%20of%20adults%20overall.
46. https://www.americanimmigrationcouncil.org/research/the-belonging-barometer?emci=c9285396-05bd-ed11-a8e0-00224832e811&emdi=ea000000-0000-0000-0000-000000000001&ceid=
47. Carey Nieuwhof Podcast with guest Lee Strobel, citing Gary

Notes

Poole's research from Seeker Groups, aired April 30, 2024. https://open.spotify.com/episode/0xLV042B6m2B0FE825i6z-K?si=1e32f8571fca4c17

CHAPTER 7

48. https://www.spurgeon.org/resource-library/sermons/soul-winning/
49. https://www.christianpost.com/news/two-thirds-of-christians-dont-know-methods-for-sharing-jesus.html
50. https://www.barna.com/research/sharing-faith-increasingly-optional-christians
51. https://www.barna.com/research/millennials-oppose-evangelism/
52. https://www.columbiadoctors.org/news/screen-time-alternatives-kids
53. https://www.cru.org/us/en/train-and-grow/transferable-concepts/be-a-fruitful-witness.4.html
54. This was a sermon that I was listening to from Greg that I was unable to find in his sermon archives
55. https://www.christianpost.com/news/two-thirds-of-christians-dont-know-methods-for-sharing-jesus.html
56. https://churchtrainer.com/the-power-of-an-invite

CONCLUSION

57. 2021 Alpha Film Series, Episode 14: Why and How Should I Tell Others. https://youtu.be/qssUveO6TEk?si=DxCHdgNWlPgN

Meet Jesse Stirnemann

An encounter with Jesus at 17 years old shifted Jesse's focus from the tennis court to the church. He turned down several college tennis scholarship offers to pursue ministry and started leading a young adult group at 19 years old. While there have been lots of twists and turns, he has been preaching the Gospel in a variety of contexts since he was called into the ministry during his senior year of high school.

He likes good coffee, good jokes and seeing people's eyes opened to the Gospel for the first time. He grew up just outside Detroit and earned a Biblical Studies degree from Rochester University in Rochester Hills, Michigan.

After working as a youth pastor and grief counselor in Metro Detroit for about a decade, he now serves as a staff pastor at Harvest Ridge Church in North Ridgeville, Ohio. Jesse enjoys serving the local church, preaching the Gospel, and training believers to share Jesus with confidence. He and his wife, Rachel, have five children and live in North Ridgeville, Ohio just a few minutes from their church.

Stay connected with Jesse at **anyonecanevangelize.com**

www.ingramcontent.com/pod-product-compliance
Lightning Source LLC
Chambersburg PA
CBHW060521080526
44586CB00012B/559